MW01130854

Penny Haren's
Pieced Appliqué™

Landauer Books

Penny Haren's
Pieced Appliqué™

Copyright© 2008 by Landauer Corporation

Pieced Appliqué™ projects
Copyright© 2008 by Penny Haren

This book was designed, produced, and published by
Landauer Books
A division of Landauer Corporation
3100 101st Street, Urbandale, IA 50322
www.landauercorp.com   800/557-2144

President/Publisher: Jeramy Lanigan Landauer
Director of Operations: Kitty Jacobson
Managing Editor: Jeri Simon
Art Director: Laurel Albright
Technical Illustrator: Linda Bender
Photographer: Craig Anderson Photography

All rights reserved. No part of this book may be
reproduced or transmitted in any form by any means,
electronic or mechanical, including photocopying,
recording, or by any information storage and
retrieval system without permission in writing from the
publisher, except as noted. The publisher presents the
information in this book in good faith. No warranty is
given, nor are results guaranteed.

ISBN 13: 978-0-9793711-9-6
ISBN 10:   0-9793711-9-8

Library of Congress Control Number: 2008926901

This book printed on acid-free paper.
Printed in China

10-9-8-7-6-5-4-3-2

Foreword

For more than 20 years as a quilter and several years as a shop owner, I've been developing and teaching techniques that make it quick, easy and fun for quilters—even beginners—to create intricate miniature blocks. But, don't let the word "miniature" intimidate you. These same techniques can be used for all of your piecing and appliqué projects —with stunning results.

Now, with this first in a series of books, I'm thrilled to be sharing these new techniques named Pieced Appliqué™ with quilters worldwide. If you're like the thousands of women I've taught, you may never look at a block pattern quite the same way again.

Pieced Appliqué™ eliminates inset points and curves from even the most complicated blocks. Quilts and blocks you may never have considered are now not only possible but a breeze.

Also, first and foremost, as a proud mother of five, I've always appreciated new tools that help save time while making quilting even easier. So I designed new fussy cutting and squaring up rulers for Creative Grids® that are perfect complements for Pieced Appliqué™.

I used three very different and unique fabric lines in this book to illustrate the dramatic difference fabric can make in a block or quilt. The LaBelle Rose line by Holly Holderman for LakeHouse Dry Goods is used in the featured Pieced Appliqué™ blocks and in the technique notebooks. The Full Sun fabric line designed by WillowBerry Lane for Maywood Fabrics and the New Nation line by Nancy Gere for Windham Fabrics are used in the color option block samples.

If you would like an exact replication of the Pieced Appliqué™ blocks, go to www.landauercorp.com for a complete list of fabrics used in each block. The paper templates can be downloaded from the Landauer web site. Be sure to compare the size of the templates you have downloaded to the templates in the book to ensure accuracy.

Enjoy the "wow" of Pieced Appliqué™ techniques. It's my joy to share these with you. You may reach me with any questions or for information about class schedules at pennyharen.com

Love,
Penny

Book Dedication

Rosemary Haueisen

The true joy of quilting

is that it is a passion that crosses all generations. Through quilting, I have become close friends with women who are twenty years younger and have been blessed to be "adopted" by three women who are twenty years older and who have become my mothers. Their generosity of spirit and zest for life always makes me smile.

Rosemary Haueisen who lost her battle with cancer just days before I was offered a job at Checker Distributers is my guardian angel. Rosemary wanted me to open a quilt shop, teach, design, and write—and she encouraged me every step of the way. Rosie taught me to embrace life, speak up and take risks. She didn't know the meaning of politically correct—and that was the joy of her spirit. She was always straight forward—and took the risk to say what everyone was thinking. She never let us ignore the elephant in the middle of the room—she made us embrace it, deal with it, and move on! I still think of her every day and can't wait to see what she has in store for me. With her pulling the strings, all my dreams come true.

Jed Hanrahan & Rae Howard

Rae Howard is the sweetest, kindest woman I have ever known. When you walk into her house, it is like stepping back in time. There is not a problem that can't be solved while sitting around her kitchen table talking and sharing. She has been waging her own battle with cancer for several years and handles it all with such dignity and grace—she is an inspiration to us all.

Rae has taught me that when you are facing life-changing challenges every day, the only thing that really matters is love. Her family, friends and one "adopted" daughter are truly blessed to be embraced by that love—and we are all better for it.

And then there's Jed Hanrahan. At 85, she has an amazing zest for life and laughter. She lives in the moment—and embraces every day. Her strength and determination have inspired us all.

Last year she had a stroke but was determined to continue to quilt. She spent days binding a quilt for my daughter—by hand—when she had lost the use of her right side. A quilt was never a greater gift.

When the doctors told us that she would never sew again, she just smiled—and adapted her sewing machine to her needs. She has made at least a dozen quilts since. When they told her she would never walk, she continued to exercise—and can now take a few steps on her own! She doesn't know the meaning of no. Now she wants to finish her Dear Jane quilt—and why not—she's not planning on going anywhere…..

These three women, who first and foremost were the matriarchs of their families, have encouraged me to dream, to embrace life, and to treasure my family. They have enriched my life. They are my joy.

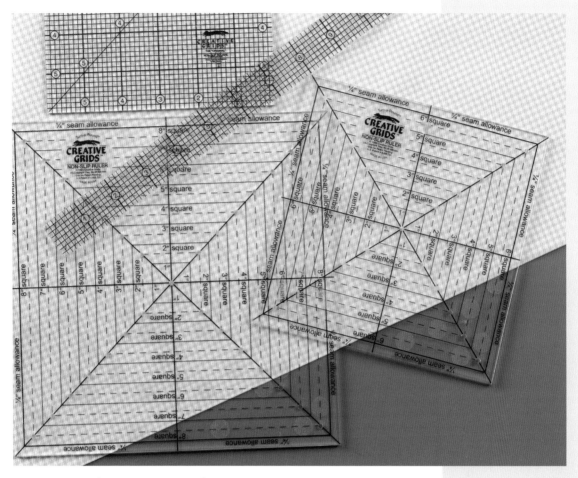

Creative Grid® Miniature Ruler Set

The 6" square ruler in this set has 1/8" solid lines which make it easy to cut small pieces accurately. The diagonal line on the ruler is great for trimming half-square triangles.

Add-A-Quarter™ Ruler

This ruler, which was actually designed for paper-piecing, has a 1/4" raised lip along one side. Butt this lip along the edge of a template to rotary cut a perfect 1/4" seam allowance every time.

Creative Grid® Square It Up & Fussy Cut Rulers

Designed to complement the Pieced Appliqué™ blocks in this book, these rulers are available in 6-1/2", 8-1/2", 9-1/2", and 12-1/2" squares. Use them to square up a block by placing the correct size of the ruler over the block to be trimmed. Match the horizontal, vertical, and diagonal lines with the seam lines of the block. The 1/4" seam is marked on the entire outside edge of the ruler so the points of your triangles won't be cut off.

The 6-1/2" square ruler was used for the Pieced Appliqué™ blocks. The 8-1/2" square ruler was used in making the pieced setting blocks in the finished quilt.

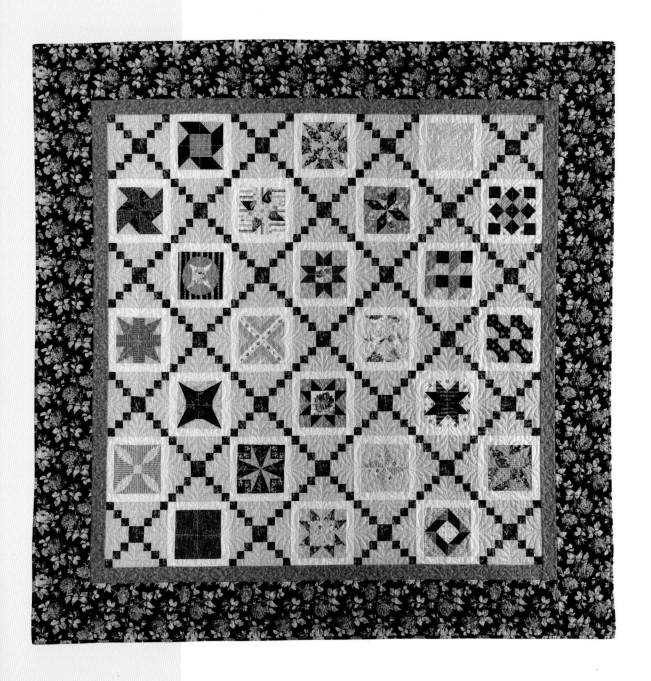

Table of Contents

General Instructions. 10

The Pieced Appliqué™ Blocks. . . 22

Lover's Knot

24

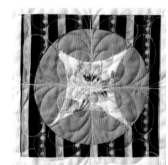

Kitty's World

26

Hummingbird

34

Bow Tie

38

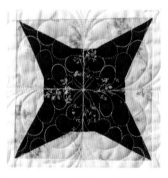

King David's Crown

42

1941 Nine-Patch

46

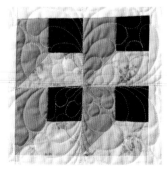

Attic Windows

52

Grandmother's Choice

54

Table of Contents

Old Windmills

58

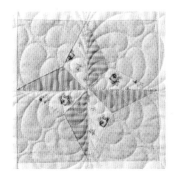

United No Longer

60

Eight-Pointed Star

62

Missouri Daisy

64

Star of the East

70

Joseph's Coat

72

Mill and Stars

78

The Arrow Star

80

Jeri's Star
82

St. Gregory's Cross
86

Sarah's Choice
90

Debby's
Nine-Patch Art
94

Boston
Uncommon
96

Sue's Hot
Cross Buns
100

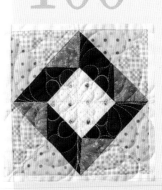

Keri's Star
104

Whirligigs
110

Windblown Square
112

Designing the Quilt 116

Everything you need to know to successfully create beautiful archival blocks you may have thought impossible is here.

Introducing Foundation Blocks

Every finished Pieced Appliqué™ block is built on an easy-to-make Foundation Block. The name of the Foundation Block you need to make for each finished block is given at the beginning of the instructions.

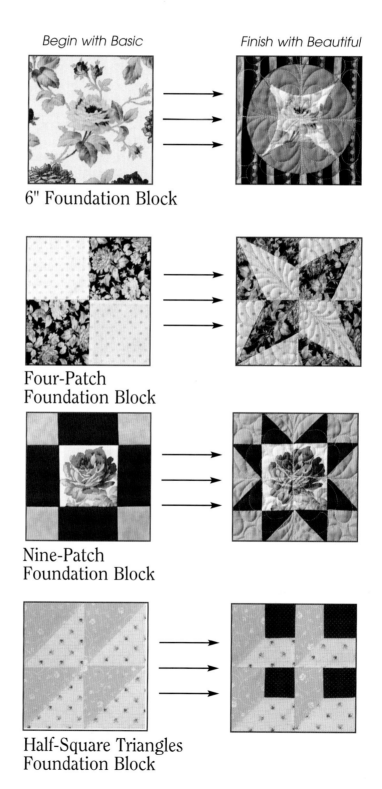

Begin with Basic   *Finish with Beautiful*

6" Foundation Block

Four-Patch
Foundation Block

Nine-Patch
Foundation Block

Half-Square Triangles
Foundation Block

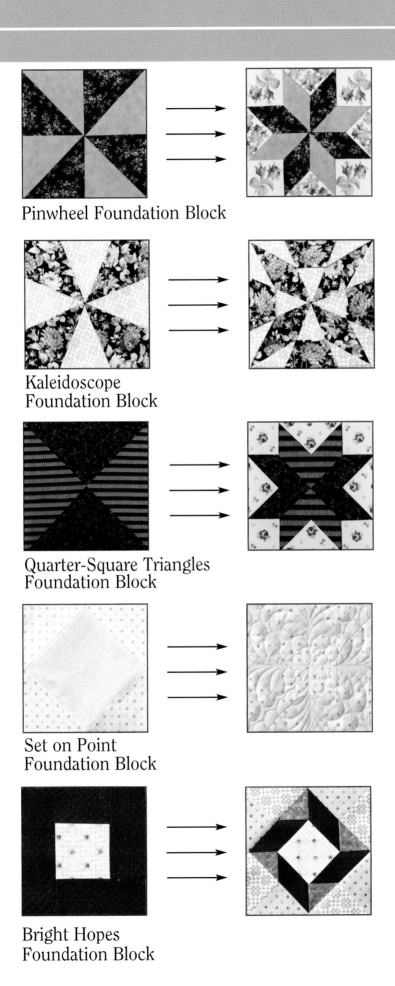

Pinwheel Foundation Block

Kaleidoscope
Foundation Block

Quarter-Square Triangles
Foundation Block

Set on Point
Foundation Block

Bright Hopes
Foundation Block

To create the Pieced Appliqué™ blocks on the following pages, you will need approximately 18 fat quarters— 6 each of neutral, medium, and dark. This is only an estimation. Fussy cutting will affect the yardage needed. You may also use an assortment of scraps, fat eighths, and fat quarters if you prefer more variety in your finished quilt. Turn the page to begin. Enjoy!

Introducing Pieced Appliqué™

Pieced Appliqué™ is an innovative new technique to create traditional pieced blocks with more accuracy and ease than the current methods. Even a beginner can create complicated blocks—even miniature blocks—with excellent results.

With Pieced Appliqué™

- You see exactly what your finished block will look like before anything is stitched.
- You control and match points and curves exactly without machine piecing.
- You create blocks with very sharp points and curves that are impossible to achieve with traditional methods.
- You eliminate puckers and inset points.
- You can carry your blocks with you to work on wherever you go.

Creating Pieced Applique™ Blocks in 5 Easy Steps

1 **Creating an easy foundation block**

2 **Making paper templates and adding freezer paper**

3 **Applying fabric and turning the appliqué using the prepared freezer paper template**

4 **Stitching the appliqué template(s) to the foundation block to create the desired archival block**

5 **Removing the paper template by soaking, drying, and pressing to finish**

The Pieced Appliqué™ Process

Making the Foundation Blocks:
The first step in the Pieced Appliqué™ process is making your foundation block.

Making Paper Templates:
To make the paper templates for your appliqués, either photocopy the template patterns shown with the block instructions or trace the template patterns onto white typing paper.

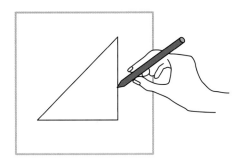

TIP

Some copiers distort images more than others. Check your copies for accuracy by comparing your templates to the templates in the book. If your copier distorts the pattern too much, you will have to trace the pattern onto white typing paper or find another copier. My own copier tends to distort in one direction about 1/16". I can live with that.

Make sure that the ink from your copies will not bleed and discolor the fabric when wet. We have not had any problems with this yet, but there is always that chance. Better safe than sorry.

• Adding Freezer Paper:
  Place the paper side of the freezer paper on top of the **blank** side of the traced or photocopied paper pattern so the iron does not smear the ink on the copy. This way, when you iron the paper pattern and freezer paper together, there's no chance of smearing the photocopied or drawn lines. With the waxy side down, iron the freezer paper to the **blank** side of the copied paper templates. Freezer paper is available at grocery stores in the paper products aisle.

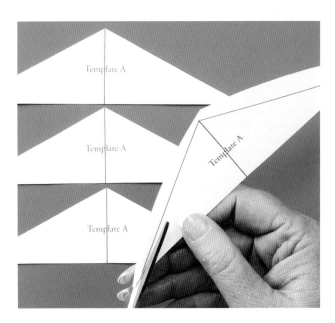

• Cutting Out the Templates:
  Cut out the templates. Be sure to cut just **inside** photocopied (or drawn) lines to allow for the thickness of the fabric when turning the fabric to make the appliqué.

13

General Instructions

Preparing and Cutting the Fabric Appliqué

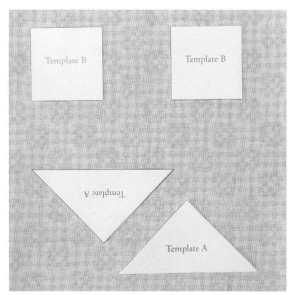

Glue the **blank** side of the freezer paper template onto the wrong side of the fabric. The printing on the freezer paper template should be face up.

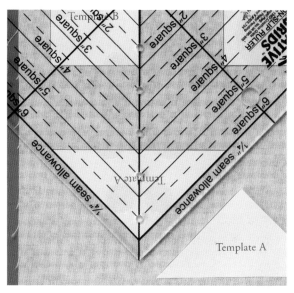

Place the ruler on the triangle and measure to provide for a 1/4" seam allowance. Using a rotary cutter, trim the fabric 1/4" away from the paper template on all sides. If you are using the Creative Grid® *Square It Up & Fussy Cut* ruler, the 1/4" seam is marked for you.

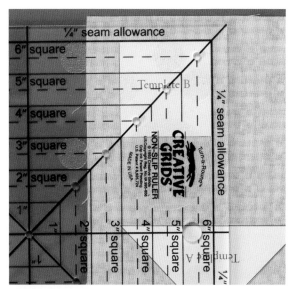

Place the ruler on each side of the square and measure to provide for a 1/4" seam allowance.

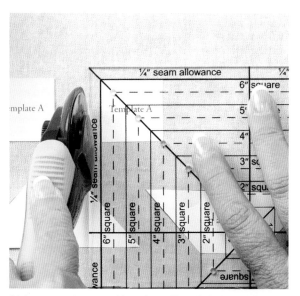

Using a rotary cutter, trim the fabric 1/4" away from the paper template on all sides. If you are using the Creative Grid® *Square It Up & Fussy Cut* ruler, the 1/4" seam is marked for you.

Turning the Appliqués
Turning Straight Edges and Corners:

Run a glue stick on the paper template and the edge of the fabric. Be sure to run the glue past the template into the seam allowance.

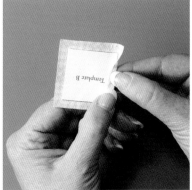

Turn the edge of the wrong side of the fabric over the template with your thumbnail moving forward 1/8" at a time. At the corner turn the fabric so it is angled slightly down.

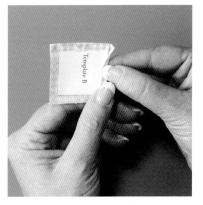

When the right angle is turned, the seam allowance for the second side will be totally hidden by the template.

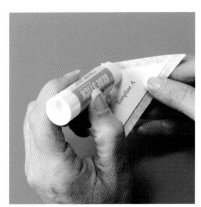

When turning a triangle, glue and turn the two sides just like a square.

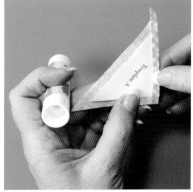

This will create "tails" on the bottom raw edge of the triangle.

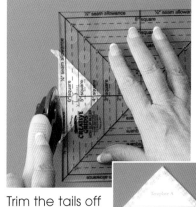

Trim the tails off even with the seam allowance.

TIP

I use white paste glue sticks to turn my appliqués. Don't purchase the purple, pink, and blue ones. You don't want to risk dyes coming back at a later date. Buy the large packages of glue sticks and keep them in the refrigerator. The moist environment stops them from drying out and they will last up to a year. When you are not using your glue stick, put the lid back on. They dry out very quickly if you leave the top off while turning each piece.

Turning the Appliqués

Turning Outside Curves:

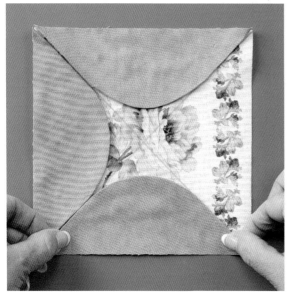

Turning Inside Curves:

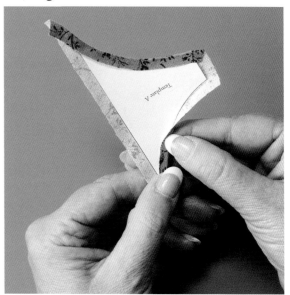

Some blocks have appliqués with curves. When turning a curved edge, gather the excess fabric around the template. Do not pleat it. If you have rough edges on your appliqué, turn it over. You will notice there are pleats on the folded edge of your piece. While the glue is still wet, place a fingernail on each side of the "pleat" and pull it down to the correct shape. In this case, when the curved appliqués are placed on the foundation block, they will touch on the diagonal.

When turning an inside curve, trim approximately 1/4" away from the curved sides. The inside curve of this appliqué does not have to be clipped. Since it is a gentle curve and the straight side of the template is placed on the grain line of the fabric, the curve is automatically placed on the bias, and turns easily with no clipping required.

TIP

Clip inside points and curves to within a few threads of the template to aid in turning. Do not clip outside curves. Every cut is a potential weakness in your project.

Turning Inner Circles:

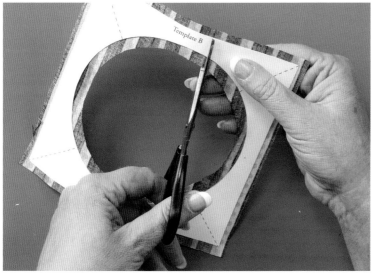

In the example above, the center circle must be cut out 1/4" away from the inner circle of the template. The seam allowance must be clipped in order to turn the fabric over the template. The fabric is trimmed exactly 1/4" away from the outside edges of the template.

After gluing the paper template and the edge of the fabric turn the edge of the wrong side of the fabric over the template with your thumbnail moving forward 1/8" at a time.

Turning one appliqué over another:

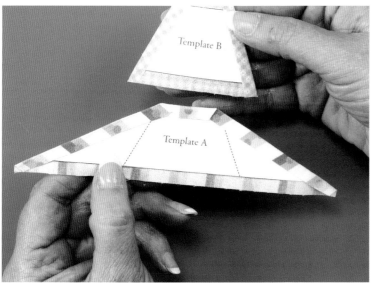

In this example, the wrong side of template B is glued to the right side of template A.

Some blocks require one appliqué to be placed on top of another.

The raw edge of template B is then turned over the top edge of template A.

General Instructions

Cutting Appliqués from a Pieced Block

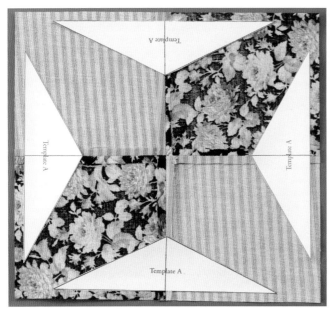

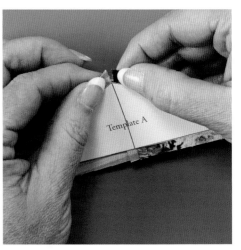

Tear out a few stitches of the seam to aid in turning the appliqué.

Some of the Pieced Appliqué™ blocks require you to make two foundation blocks. One of the blocks will be used to cut the appliqués, as demonstrated in the photo above. Place the lines on the paper template on the seam lines of the wrong side of the pieced block and trim 1/4" away from the templates on all sides.

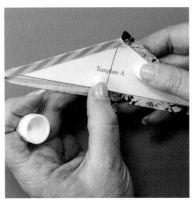

Glue and turn one side of the appliqué, and then the other.

Run glue on the wrong side of the template. Matching the seam lines, glue the appliqué in place on the foundation block.

Rotate the block as you place the appliqués. Since the appliqués were trimmed exactly 1/4" away from the templates, the raw edges should be placed even with the raw edges of the four-patch.

TIP

Do not glue the fabric of the seam allowance. You don't want to stitch through it later.

18

Stitching the Appliqué Templates
Thread

Use only high quality cotton thread or cotton wrapped polyester. There is a difference; not all threads are created equal.

 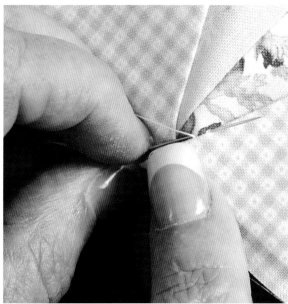

Hand stitch the turned edges of the appliqué, using an invisible appliqué stitch. Leave the raw edges open. If your appliqué pieces are layered only stitch to the fabric directly below. Do not go clear down to the foundation block. You don't want to sew the paper templates into your work. Take a few extra stitches to reinforce any areas that were clipped because of inside curves. Knots should be hidden beneath the appliqué piece. Do not place your knot on the wrong side of the foundation square. The thread tail could shadow through the finished block.

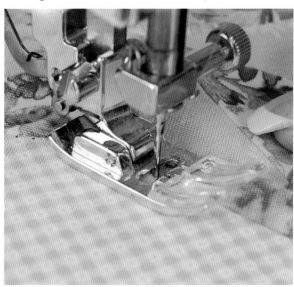 

If you prefer to machine stitch, use a narrow zigzag stitch with invisible thread in the top of your machine and regular 50 or 60 weight thread in the bobbin. If your appliqué pieces are layered, stitch the bottom appliqué first. Remove the paper templates and press your block. Glue the second layer of appliqués to your block and stitch them in place. Remove the paper templates and press.

General Instructions

Removing the Paper Templates and Glue

When the stitching is done, place the appliquéd block into warm water for at least twenty minutes. This will dissolve the glue.

Remove the appliquéd block from the water and squeeze out the excess water.

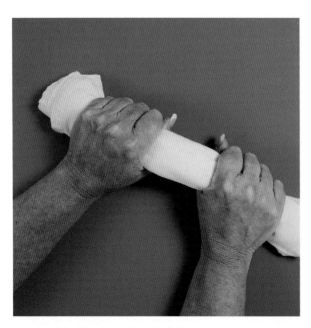

Roll the block in an absorbent towel to remove any remaining water.

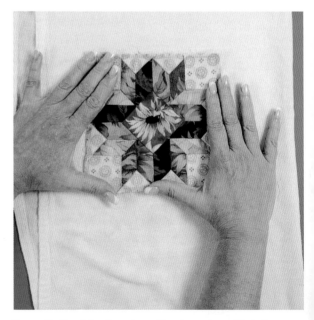

Smooth the block out on the towel and let dry before removing the paper templates.

Pull out the paper templates along the raw edges of the block. Run the seams under water to flush out any remaining glue.

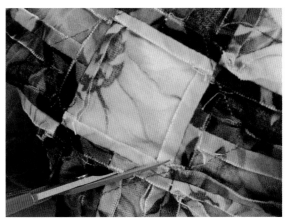

To remove inside templates slit or cut the background fabric. Avoid cutting through the appliquéd stitches

Remove the inside paper templates. You may also cut away any excess fabric, if you wish.

Smooth the block out again and press.

TIP

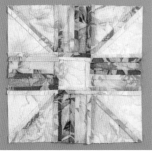

Press the seams open when sewing your foundation block. The block will lay flat making the appliqués easier to line up and place.

TIP

Press your appliquéd blocks on a folded bath towel. The towel absorbs the seams so that there is no "shadow" created by the seams on the front of the piece. I spray each piece with spray starch and press the wrong side to guarantee that all of the seams are pressed correctly. Then I press the right side. The spray starch gives it a crisp look, reduces distortion and fraying, and protects the finished block.

The Pieced Appliqué™ Blocks

Lover's Knot

6" Foundation Block

Light Print Fabric:
6-1/2" Square

Dark Print Fabric:
Scraps to Cut 4 of Appliqué A

*Refer to General Instructions on pages 10-21
before beginning this block.*

CUTTING THE PAPER TEMPLATE

Cut four of Template A.

PIECING

This block consists of 5 pieces.

1 Cut the 6-1/2" square from the light print.

2 Glue the A paper templates to the wrong side of a scrap of dark print fabric. Trim the fabric EXACTLY 1/4" away from the straight side of each template. Do not turn this side. Trim the fabric approximately 1/4" away from all three curved edges of each template. Turn the curved edges.

3 Glue the wrong side of the appliqués in place on the #1 light print square. The raw edges of the appliqués should be placed even with the raw edges of the light print square.

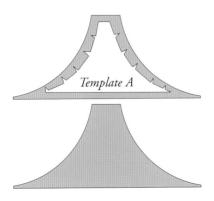

Template A

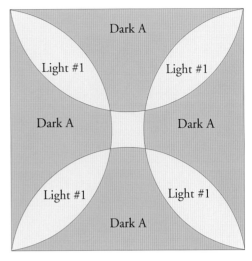

4 Appliqué in place, leaving raw edges open. Follow directions on pages 20-21 to remove paper templates and glue. Press.

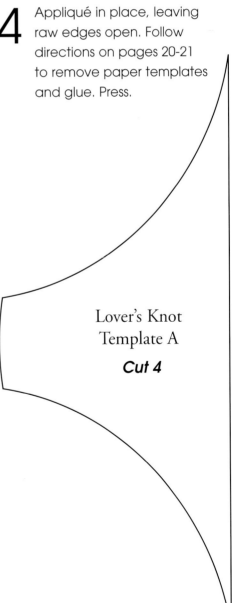

Lover's Knot
Template A
Cut 4

Kitty's World

6" Foundation Block

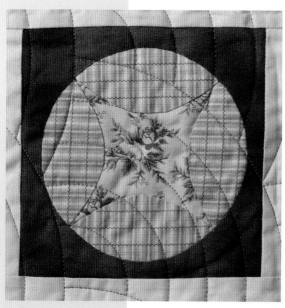

Light Print Fabric:
6-1/2" Square

Medium Print Fabric:
Scraps to Cut 4 of Appliqué A

Dark Print Fabric:
Scrap to Cut 1 of Appliqué B

Refer to General Instructions on pages 10-21 before beginning this block.

CUTTING THE PAPER TEMPLATES

Cut four of Template A, page 28, and one of Template B. The B Template is reverse appliquéd. Therefore, you must cut out the center circle.

PIECING

This block consists of 6 pieces.

1 Cut the 6-1/2" square from the light print.

2 Glue the four A paper templates to the wrong side of a scrap of medium print fabric. Trim the fabric EXACTLY 1/4" away from the straight side of each template. Do not turn this side. Trim the fabric approximately 1/4" away from the curved edge of each template. Turn the curved edge.

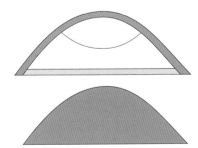

3 Glue the wrong side of the A appliqués in place on the right side of the #1 light print square. The raw edges of the appliqués should be

placed even with the raw edges of the light print square.

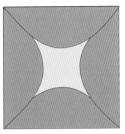

4 Glue the B paper template to the wrong side of a scrap of dark print fabric. Trim the fabric EXACTLY 1/4" away from the straight sides of the template. Do not turn these sides. Trim the fabric approximately 1/4" away from the inside circle. Clip and turn the inside circle.

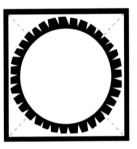

5 Glue the wrong side of the B appliqué in place on the #1 light print square. The raw edges of the appliqué should be placed even with the raw edges of the #1 light print square.

6 Appliqué in place, leaving raw edges open. Follow directions on pages 20-21 to remove paper templates and glue. Press.

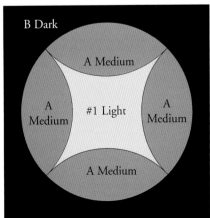

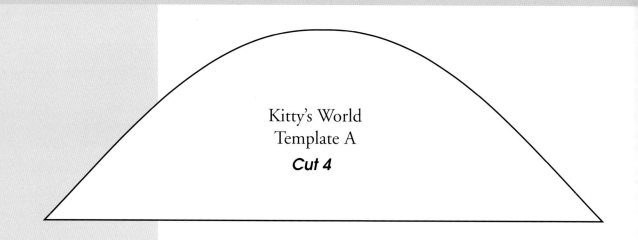

Kitty's World
Template A
Cut 4

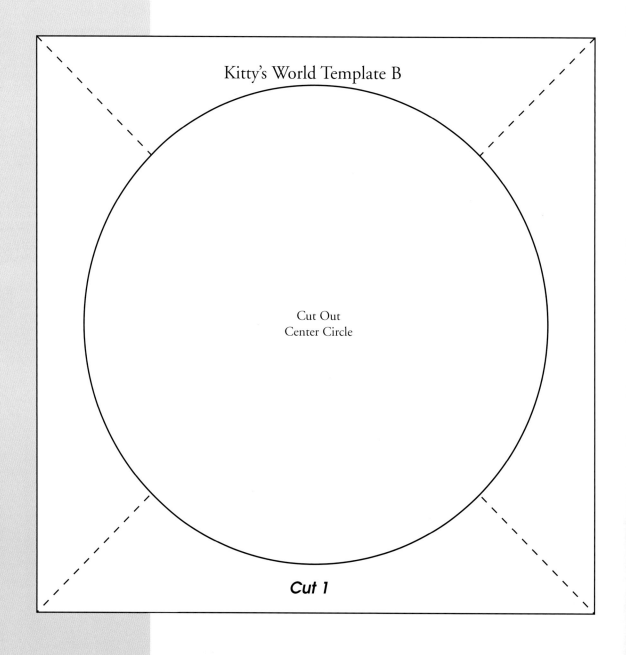

Kitty's World Template B

Cut Out
Center Circle

Cut 1

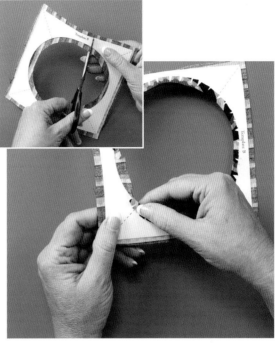

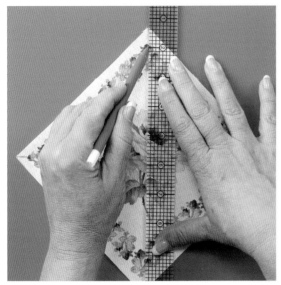

MARK THE SQUARE

Draw a diagonal line in both directions with a water soluble marker to aid in placement of the curved templates. The markings will also be useful if you are fussy cutting your square.

CLIP THE INSIDE CIRCLE

Clip the fabric at the inside circle of the template. This will aid in turning the fabric to the wrong side. If the straight edge of the template is placed on the straight of grain, there is no need to clip the curved edges to turn. The edges will "stretch" to turn.

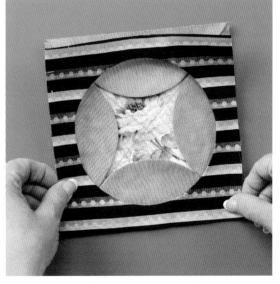

PLACE THE CURVED APPLIQUÉS

Glue the wrong side of the curved appliqués in place on the right side of the foundation square. The raw edges of the appliqués should be placed even with the raw edges of the block.

PLACE THE CIRCLE APPLIQUÉ

Place the glued side of the circle appliqué on the foundation block. Align the raw edges of the appliqué and the block. Stitch the inner circle and curved appliqués in place.

Four-Patch Foundation Block

A four-patch is a block that consists of four squares of equal size. All of the four-patches in this book were made using this method.

Two squares of contrasting fabrics will make two four-patches. The squares must be cut at least 1" larger than the finished size of the block.

If you need a 6" finished four-patch, for instance, cut the squares at least 7". After sewing, the four-patches should measure 6-1/2". This includes the seam allowances.

I prefer to cut the squares 2" larger so that I can trim the four-patches to the correct size after the sewing is complete. Make a sample block to learn the technique before cutting the fabric for your quilt.

FABRICS

Cut 1—8" Square of a Light Fabric

Cut 1—8" Square of a Dark Fabric

PIECING

1 Place the light fabric square, right sides together, on top of the dark fabric square.

Note: Use spray starch to iron the squares together.

2 Sew a 1/4" seam along two opposite sides of the squares using a matching cotton thread. Clip all threads.

3 Cut this unit in half, parallel to the sewn seams. Each strip should measure 4". Press the seams open.

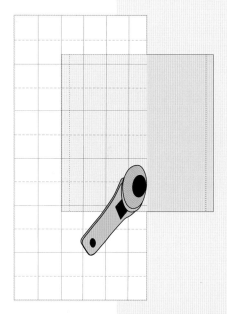

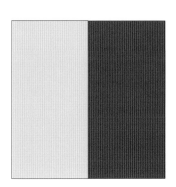

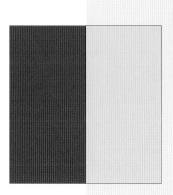

4 Place these two units, right sides together, with the dark fabric strip on top of the light fabric strip. Match the seams.

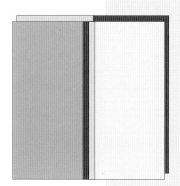

Four-Patch Foundation Block

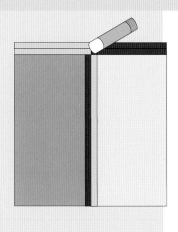

5 Place a dab of glue 1/4" in from the outer edge and line up the seam allowances. Any dab of glue that shows on the front of the block can easily be washed away. Place a dab of glue 1/4" in from the other edge and line up the seam allowances.

Note: *The glue will ensure that the center seams of your four-patches will match perfectly.*

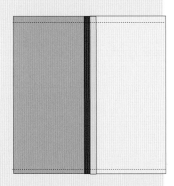

6 Sew a 1/4" seam along the two opposite sides that are perpendicular to the sewn seams.

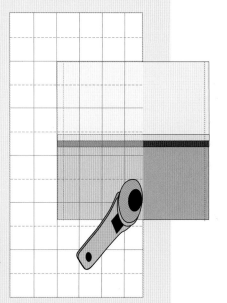

7 Cut this unit in half, parallel to the sewn seams. Each strip should measure 4". Press the seams open.

8 Place the 6-1/2" Square It Up Ruler on top of the four-patch, placing the horizontal and vertical lines on the seam lines of the four-patch. Trim the outside edge of the block.

Note: In most cases, one four-patch will be used as the foundation block and will be trimmed to 6-1/2". Appliqués will be cut from the other four-patch, so it should not be trimmed.

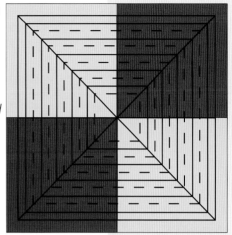

You now have two completed four-patch units.

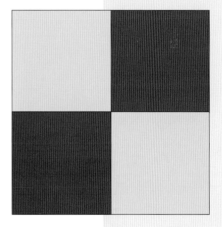

Hummingbird

Four-Patch Foundation Block

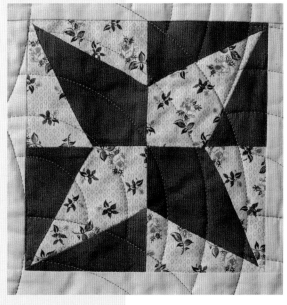

FABRICS

Light Print Fabric:
1—9" Square

Dark Print Fabric:
1—9" Square

Refer to General Instructions on pages 10-21 before beginning this block.

CUTTING THE PAPER TEMPLATE

Cut four of Template A on page 36. The fabric for the A appliqués will be cut from one of the four-patches.

Note: *By placing and cutting the A templates from a pieced four-patch block, the raw edge of the appliqué is on the straight of the grain of the fabric so the finished block is more stable.*

The fabrics for two of the appliqués are mirror images of the other two appliqués. Since the appliqués are cut from a completed four-patch, these are automatically reversed for you.

Only one center of a four-patch will show in the finished block, so save the "best" four-patch for the foundation block.

PIECING

This block consists of 12 pieces.

1 Following the four-patch foundation block directions on page 30, make two four-patches with the #1 light print fabric square and the #2 dark print fabric square. The finished four-patches are oversized – they should measure approximately 8".

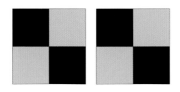

2 Glue the A paper templates to the wrong side of a four-patch, matching the drawn lines on the templates to the seam lines on the four-patch.

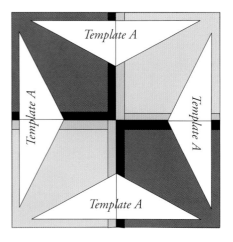

3 Trim the fabric EXACTLY 1/4" away from the templates on all sides.

4 Turn the two short sides of each appliqué. Do not turn the long side. Two appliqués will have the light fabric on the left and two will have the light fabric on the right.

5 Trim the remaining four-patch to 6-1/2" (3-1/4" from each seam).

35

6 Glue the wrong sides of the appliqués in place on the trimmed four-patch, matching the seam lines and alternating the fabrics. The raw edges of the appliqués should be placed even with the raw edges of the four-patch.

7 Appliqué in place, leaving raw edges open. Follow directions on pages 20-21 to remove paper templates and glue. Press.

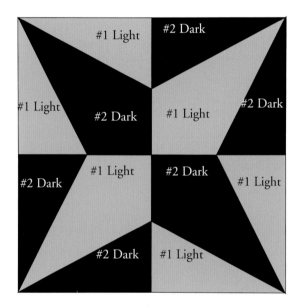

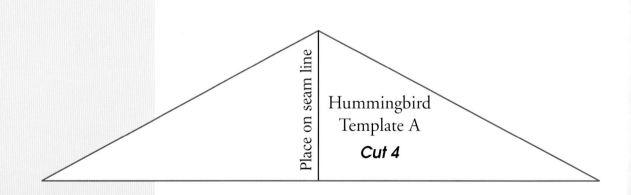

Place on seam line

Hummingbird
Template A
Cut 4

PLACE THE APPLIQUÉS

Place the prepared appliqués on the seam lines of the four-patch foundation block. Line up the raw edges of the appliqués with the raw edges of the foundation block. The fabrics should create a mirror-like image.

TRIM THE BLOCK

Trim the fabric tails of the appliqués after gluing them in place on the foundation block. Your block should measure 6-1/2". Stitch the appliqués in place, leaving raw edges open. Remove paper templates and glue, referring to pages 20-21. Press.

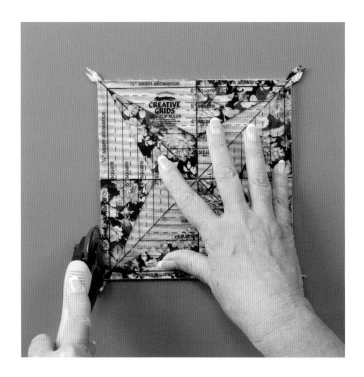

Bow Tie

Four-Patch Foundation Block

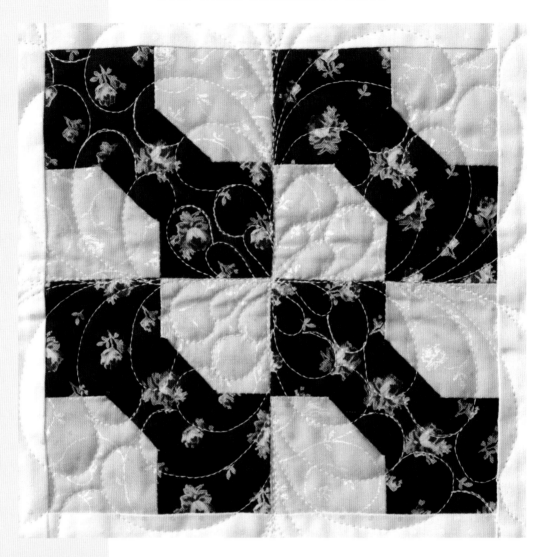

FABRICS

Light Print Fabrics:
#1—Cut 2—4-1/2" Squares

Dark Print Fabrics:
#2—Cut 2—4-1/2" Squares
Scraps to Cut 4 of Appliqué A

*Refer to General Instructions on pages 10-21
before beginning this block.*

CUTTING THE PAPER TEMPLATE

Cut four of Template A.

> Bow Tie
> Template A
> ***Cut 4***

PIECING

This block consists of 20 pieces.

1 Following the four-patch foundation
block directions on page 30, make four
four-patches with the #1 light print
fabric and the #2 dark print fabric. The
finished four-patches are oversized,
they should measure approximately 4".

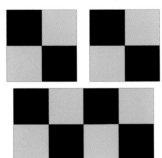

Note: *None of the centers of the four-
patches will show in the finished block,
so if the seams don't match perfectly,
don't worry about it. They will be
covered by the A appliqués.*

*By appliquéing the "knot" on the bow
tie, there are no inset points.*

2 Trim the four-patches to 3-1/2" (1-3/4"
from each seam).

3 Sew together the four, trimmed
four-patches to form a sixteen-patch
block, alternating fabrics. These seams
show, so the center seams must match.
Press the seams open.

4 Glue the A paper templates to
the wrong side of a scrap of dark
print fabric.

Template A

5 Trim the fabric EXACTLY 1/4" away from
the templates on all sides. Turn all sides
of the appliqués.

6 Glue the appliqués in place on the
pieced sixteen-patch block to form four
bow ties.

7 Appliqué in place. Remove the paper
templates and glue, following the
instructions on pages 20-21. Press.

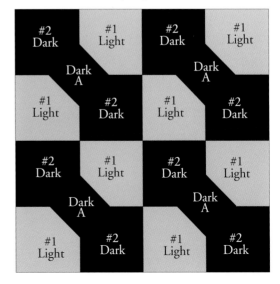

Nine-Patch Foundation Block

A nine-patch block traditionally consists of nine squares sewn in three rows of three squares. In this book, a nine-patch consists of three rows of three units. Those nine units may consist of rectangles, half-square triangles, and even nine-patches. The method is the same.

Make a sample block to learn the technique before cutting the fabric for your quilt. Measure the completed block to check your seam allowance.

The completed block should measure 6-1/2".

FABRICS

5—2-1/2" Squares of Dark Fabric

4—2-1/2" Squares of Light Fabric

PIECING

1 Lay out the nine squares in three rows of three blocks each. The dark fabric squares should be placed at the corners and in the center.

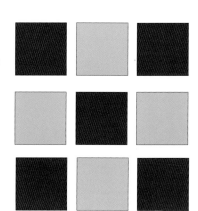

2 Place the squares in the center column – right sides together on the left-hand column. Pick up the first pair in the top left corner. Then, pick up the middle pair, then the bottom pair. The bottom pair will be on the bottom of the stack. Pick up the right-hand column from the top to the bottom in the same manner.

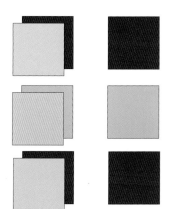

3 Pick up the top two squares, which are already right sides together, and sew the right side of the squares. Do not break the thread. Pick up the next two squares and sew the right side of these squares. Do not break the thread. Pick up the last two squares that are right sides together and sew the right side of these squares. Three squares will be left. The top square will be right side up. You have sewn three sets of two squares that are held together by threads.

4 Open the first set of squares and place the top, dark square, right sides together, on the light fabric square. Sew on the right side of the square. Do not break the thread.

5 Open the second set of squares and place the next, light square, right sides together, on the dark fabric square. Sew on the right side of the square. Do not break the thread.

6 Open the third set of squares and place the remaining dark square, right sides together, on the light fabric square. Sew on the right side of the square. Do not clip the thread. Press the seams open.

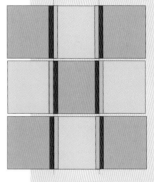

7 Place the second column, right sides together, on the first column. Match the seams. Sew this seam. Place the third column, right sides together, on the second column. Match the seams and sew this seam.

8 Clip the threads that held the rows together and press the seams open.

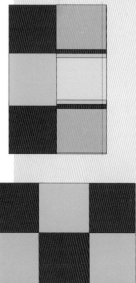

King David's Crown

Nine-Patch Foundation Block

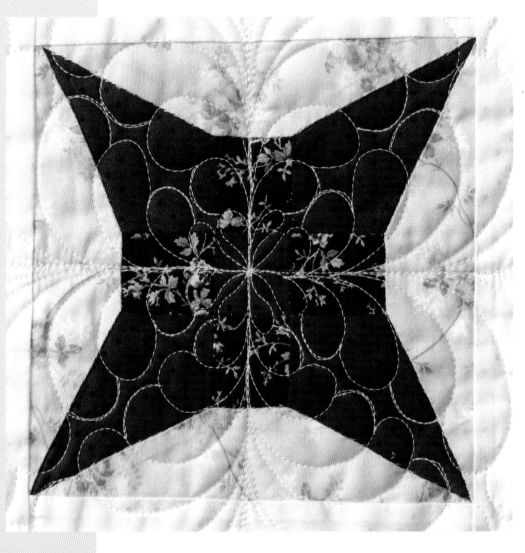

Light Print Fabric:
Scraps to Cut 4 of Appliqué A

Medium Print Fabric:
#1—Cut 1—1-1/2" Square
#2—Cut 4 – 3" Squares

Dark Print Fabric:
#3—Cut 4 – 1-1/2" x 3" Rectangles

*Refer to General Instructions on pages 10-21
before beginning this block.*

CUTTING THE PAPER TEMPLATES

Cut four of Template A on page 44.

PIECING

This block consists of 13 pieces.
> **Note:** *Try fussy cutting a striped fabric
> for the #3 dark print rectangles.*

1 Sew a #2 medium print square to opposite sides of a #3 dark print rectangle along the 3" sides. Make a total of two sets. Press the seams open.

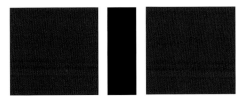

2 Sew the remaining #3 dark print rectangles to opposite sides of the #1 medium print square along the 1-1/2" sides. Press the seams open.

3 Sew the sets made in Step #1 to opposite sides of the set made in Step #2 along the 6-1/2" sides, matching seams. Press the seams open.

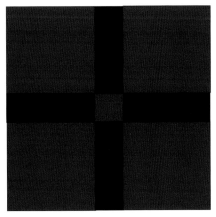

4 Glue the A paper templates to the wrong side of a scrap of light print fabric. Trim the fabric EXACTLY 1/4" away from all sides of the templates. Do not turn the longest side of each appliqué. Turn the other three sides.

Template A

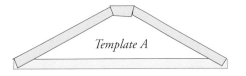

Template A

5 Glue the wrong side of the appliqués in place on the pieced foundation block. The raw edge of the appliqués should be placed even with the raw edge of the block.

6 Appliqué in place, leaving raw edges open. Follow directions on pages 20-21 to remove paper templates and glue. Press.

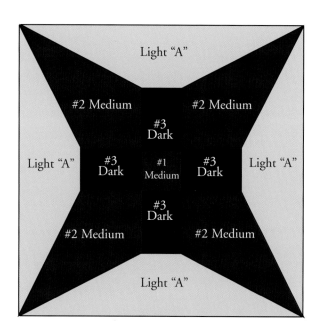

King David's Crown
Template A
Cut 4

PLACE THE APPLIQUÉS

After turning the three short sides of the template, glue the wrong side to the nine-patch foundation block. Place the raw edge of the appliqué even with the raw edge of the block.

Note: *If the top of the turned appliqué is not the same width as the rectangle, you must adjust the width of your seam allowance.*

TRIM THE TAILS

When all four appliqués have been glued and placed on the block, the corners should form perfect points. Trim the fabric tails even with the foundation block.

1941 Nine-Patch

Nine-Patch Foundation Block

Light Print Fabric:
#1—Cut 4—2-1/2" Squares

Medium Print Fabric:
#2—Cut 1—2-1/2" Square

Dark Print Fabric:
#3—Cut 4—2-1/2" Squares

Refer to General Instructions on pages 10-21 before beginning this block.

CUTTING THE PAPER TEMPLATE

Cut four of Template A.

1941
Nine-Patch
Template A
Cut 4

PIECING

This block consists of 13 pieces.
Note: *Try fussy cutting the center, medium print square.*

1 Following the nine-patch foundation block directions on page 40, make a nine-patch with the #2 medium print square (center); the #1 light print squares (corners); and the #3 dark print squares. Press the seams open.

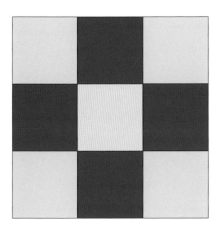

2 Glue the A paper templates to the wrong side of a scrap of light print fabric. Trim the fabric EXACTLY 1/4" away from all sides of each template. Do not turn the longest side of each template. Turn the other two sides.

Template A

3 Glue the wrong side of the appliqués in place on the pieced nine-patch block. The raw edge of the appliqués should be placed even with the raw edge of the block.

4 Appliqué in place, leaving raw edges open. Follow directions on pages 20-21 to remove paper templates and glue. Press.

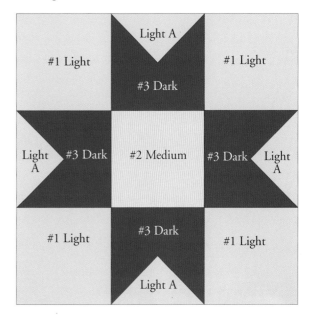

Light A
#1 Light | #1 Light
#3 Dark
Light A | #3 Dark | #2 Medium | #3 Dark | Light A
#1 Light | #3 Dark | #1 Light
Light A

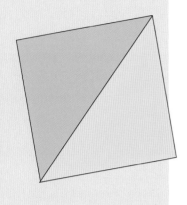

A half-square triangle is a square that consists of two ninety-degree triangles pieced on the longest side. These half-square triangles were made using two different methods.

If the half-square triangles needed to be trimmed to a different size, I used Method #1.

If the finished size of the square was 3" – 3-1/2" including the seam allowance – I used Triangles on a Roll™ paper – Method #2.

METHOD #1:

Note: Generally, when making half-square triangles, the squares should be cut 7/8" larger than the finished block. Since you are sewing bias seams, the sewing and pressing tend to distort the shape of your finished square. Therefore, I add 2" so that I can square them up to the correct size after stitching and pressing.

FABRICS

2—4" Squares of
Light Fabric

2—4" Squares of
Dark Fabric

Make a sample block to learn the technique before cutting the fabric for your quilt.

In the Grandmother's Choice block on page 54, the half-square triangles were made from 4" squares and trimmed to 2-7/8". In the following example, the fabric is cut and trimmed as if you were making the Grandmother's Choice block.

PIECING

1 Place a light fabric square, right sides together, on top of a dark fabric square. Draw a line across the diagonal. Be sure to use a pencil or a marking tool that is water soluble. Ink may bleed onto your quilt when you wash it. Repeat with the other set of squares.
Note: Draw the line from the center out in both directions so you don't wrinkle the corners.

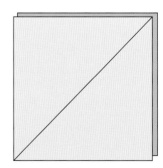

2 Stitch a seam 1/4" on each side of the drawn line. Cut on the drawn line. Repeat with the other set of squares.

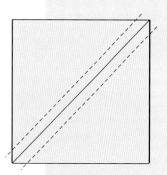

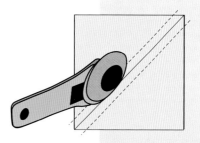

3 Open the half-square triangles and press the seams open. Each set of squares will make two half-square triangle units. These blocks will be slightly larger than 3-1/2".

4 Place the 6" Miniature Ruler on the upper left corner of the right side of the square. The diagonal line marking on the ruler should be placed on the seam line. Trim the top and left side.

5 Turn the block so the uncut edges are on the top and left side. Place the 6" Miniature Ruler so the diagonal line is placed on the seam line and the 2-7/8" markings are even with the square on the right and bottom sides. Trim the top and left side. The finished square now measures to 2-7/8".

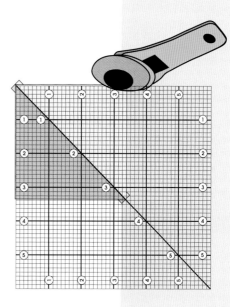

FABRICS

1—4-1/2" x 8-1/2" Rectangle of Light Fabric

1—4-1/2" x 8-1/2" Rectangle of Dark Fabric

1—Rectangle of Two Squares of 3" Triangles on a Roll™ paper

METHOD #2—Using Triangles on a Roll™:

PIECING

1 Place the 4-1/2" x 8-1/2" rectangle of light fabric on the 4-1/2" x 8-1/2" rectangle of dark fabric, right sides together. Pin the triangle paper to the fabric avoiding any printed lines. Sew on all of the dashed lines.

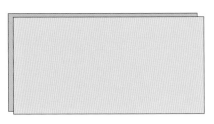

2 Cut on all of the solid lines, including the outside edges. You have made 4 half-square triangles. DO NOT REMOVE THE PAPER.

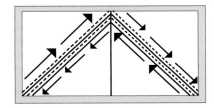

3 Place the paper side down on the ironing board and press all of the seams toward the dark fabric. The paper stabilizes the bias seam so it does not become distorted while you are pressing. Repeat for all four half-square triangles.

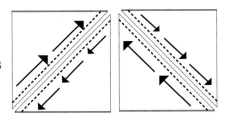

4 Trim the "tails" that stick out past the square. Remove the paper by tearing it out in both directions from the center point. Do not try to tear it away from the seamed corners or you could tear out a few of the stitches and weaken your final block. Repress the seams open. Repeat for all four half-square triangles.

FUSSY CUTTING

Many of the appliqués can be fussy cut to showcase a particular design in the fabric. This technique adds drama and eye appeal to the Pieced Appliqué™ blocks. The Creative Grid® *Square It Up & Fussy Cut* ruler makes the process quick and easy.

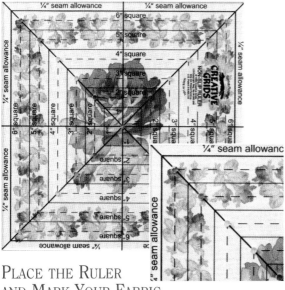

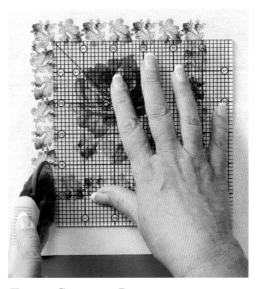

PLACE THE RULER AND MARK YOUR FABRIC

Place the ruler over the design you want to fussy cut. If a rose fits within the 4" square markings, use a water soluble pen to mark the corners of the square at 4-1/2". This includes the seam allowance.

As shown in the inset, the *Square It Up & Fussy Cut* rulers have holes where a water soluble marker can be used to mark the fabric. This insures a centered design every time.

FUSSY CUT THE DESIGN

Place the top left corner of the ruler on the top left corner dot. Line up the two sides of the ruler with the top right dot and the bottom left dot. Cut the top and left side of the fussy cut square. Turn the ruler and cut the other two sides.

FINISH THE BLOCK

When pieced in your foundation block, the rose will be centered, as in Jeri's Star.

TIP

When you are fussy cutting a design for an appliqué, center and glue the template to the wrong side of the fussy cut piece.

Triangles can be fussy cut by marking the corner and points of the triangle. Then trim the two straight sides and cut the diagonal.

Attic Windows

Half-Square Triangles Foundation Block

Light Print Fabric:
#1—Cut 1—4-1/2" x 8-1/2"
Rectangle

Medium Print Fabric:
#2—Cut 1—4-1/2" x 8-1/2"
Rectangle

Dark Print Fabric:
Scraps to Cut 4 of Appliqué A

*Refer to General Instructions on pages 10-21
before beginning this block.*

CUTTING THE PAPER TEMPLATE

Cut four of Template A.

Attic Windows
Template A
Cut 4

PIECING

This block consists of 12 pieces.

> **Note:** *Choose fabrics that will
> showcase the light, medium and
> dark aspects of the design. Picture
> the sun hitting a windowsill.*

1 Using Method #2, on page 50, and
3" Triangles on a Roll™ paper, make
four half-square triangles for the
foundation block with the #1 light
print fabric and the #2 medium print
fabric. Press the seams open.

2 Glue the A paper templates to the wrong
side of a scrap of dark print fabric. Trim
the fabric EXACTLY 1/4" away from all
sides of the templates. Turn two adjoining
sides of the appliqués.

Template A

3 Glue the wrong side of the appliqués
in place on the pieced half-square
triangles. The raw edges of the
appliqués should be placed even with
the raw edges of one corner of the
half-square triangles.

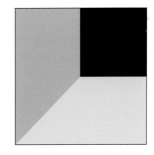

4 Appliqué in place, leaving raw edges
open. Follow directions on pages 20-21 to
remove paper templates and glue. Press.

5 Sew these four half-square triangles
together to form the finished block.
Press the seams open.

#2 Medium	Dark "A"	#2 Medium	Dark "A"
Light #1		Light #1	
#2 Medium	Dark "A"	#2 Medium	Dark "A"
Light #1		Light #1	

53

Grandmother's Choice

Half-Square Triangles Foundation Block

FABRICS

Light Print Fabric:
#1—Cut 2—4" Squares

#2—Cut 4—1-3/4" x 2-7/8" Rectangles

Medium Print Fabric:
#3—Cut 1—1-3/4" Square

Dark Print Fabric:
#4—Cut 2—4" Squares
Scraps to Cut 4 of Appliqué A

Refer to General Instructions on pages 10-21 before beginning this block.

CUTTING THE PAPER TEMPLATE

Cut four of Template A.

> Grandmother's
> Choice
> Template A
>
> **Cut 4**

PIECING

This block consists of 17 pieces.

> **Note:** *I prefer to use triangle paper when making half-square triangles. But, in this case, the half-square triangles need to be cut down to an odd size so I used Method #1. Try fussy cutting the center medium print square.*

1 Using Method #1, on page 48 make four half-square triangles with the #1 light print fabric and the #4 dark print fabric. Press the seams open. Trim these half-square triangles to 2-7/8" squares.

2 Following the half-square triangles foundation block directions on page 48 make a nine-patch with the #1 medium print square (center); the trimmed half-square triangles (corners); and the #2 light print rectangles. Press the seams open.

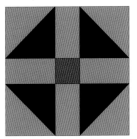

3 Glue the A paper templates to the wrong side of a scrap of dark print fabric. Trim the fabric EXACTLY 1/4" away from all sides of the templates. Turn two adjoining sides of the appliqués.

Template A

4 Glue the wrong side of the appliqués in place on the pieced half-square triangles. The raw edges of the appliqués should be placed even with the raw edges of the foundation block.

5 Appliqué in place, leaving raw edges open. Follow directions on pages 20-21 to remove paper templates and glue. Press.

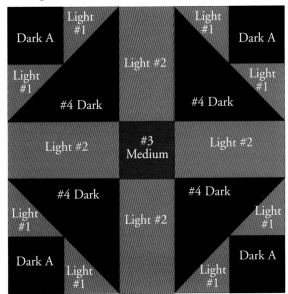

Pinwheel Foundation Block

A pinwheel is made from four half-square triangles.

Make a sample block to learn the technique before cutting the fabric for your quilt.

PIECING

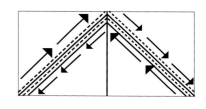

1 Using Method #2, page 50, make four half-square triangles with 3" Triangles on a Roll™ paper.

FABRICS

1—4-1/2" x 8-1/2" Rectangle of Light Fabric

1—4-1/2" x 8-1/2" Rectangle of Dark Fabric

1—Rectangle of Two Squares of 3" Triangles on a Roll™ paper

2 Lay out the four half-square triangles to form a pinwheel. It is possible to sew a mirror image of this block and have the blades of your pinwheel "blowing" in the other direction. Be careful.

3 Place the half-square triangles in the second column, right sides together, over the first column, matching the seams. Place a dab of glue on the seam so it doesn't shift while sewing.

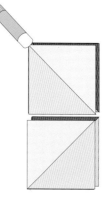

4 Sew these seams, one after the other, by chain-piecing them on the sewing machine.

5 Press the seams open. Check and make sure that the points of the triangles match 1/4" in from the outer edge. If they do not match now, the center of the pinwheel will not match after the final seam is sewn.

6 Place the right column over the left column, right sides together, matching the center seam. Use a dab of glue to make sure that nothing shifts when stitching. Sew this final seam. Press the seam open.

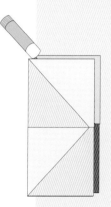

Old Windmills

Pinwheel Foundation Block

Light Print Fabric:
Scraps to Cut 4 of Appliqué A

Medium Print Fabric:
#1—Cut 1—4 -1/2" x 8-1/2"
Rectangle

Dark Print Fabric:
#2—Cut 1—4 -1/2" x 8-1/2"
Rectangle

*Refer to General Instructions on pages 10-21
before beginning this block.*

CUTTING THE PAPER TEMPLATE

Cut four of Template A.

PIECING

This block consists of 12 pieces.
Note: *Choose fabrics that will
showcase the dark print pinwheel.*

1 Using Method #2, on page 50, and 3"
Triangles on a Roll™ paper , make
four half-square triangles with the #1
medium print fabric and the #2 dark
print fabric. Press all seams open.

2 Following the pinwheel foundation
block directions on page 56, make a
pinwheel from the four half-square
triangles. Press all seams open.

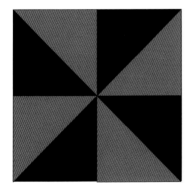

3 Glue the A paper templates to the
wrong side of a scrap of light print
fabric. Trim the fabric EXACTLY
1/4" away from all sides of the
templates. Turn the two, short sides
of the appliqués.

4 Glue the wrong side of the appliqués
in place on the pieced pinwheel
block. The raw edge of the appliqués
should be placed even with the raw
edge of the dark print side of the
half-square triangles.

5 Appliqué in place, leaving raw edges
open. Follow directions on pages 20-21
to remove paper templates and
glue. Press.

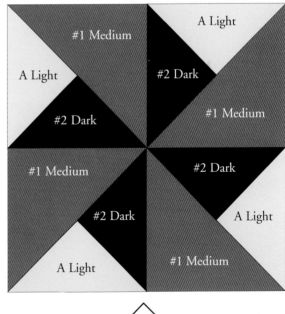

Old Windmills
Template A

Cut 4

United No Longer

Pinwheel Foundation Block

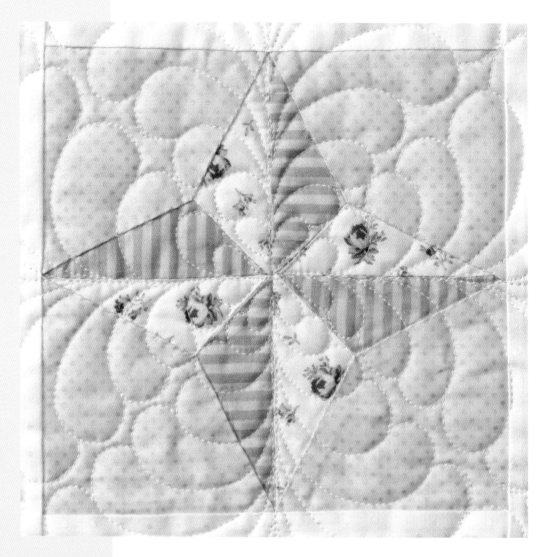

Light Print Fabric:
Scraps to Cut 4 of Appliqué A

Medium Print Fabric:
#1—Cut 1—4-1/2" x 8-1/2"
Rectangle

Dark Print Fabric:
#2—Cut 1—4-1/2" x 8-1/2"
Rectangle

Refer to General Instructions on pages 10-21 before beginning this block.

CUTTING THE PAPER TEMPLATE

Cut four of Template A.

PIECING

This block consists of 12 pieces.

1 Using Method #2, on page 50, and 3" Triangles on a Roll™ paper, make four half-square triangles with the #1 medium print fabric and the #2 dark print fabric. Press all seams open.

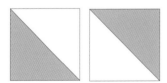

2 Follow the pinwheel foundation block directions on page 56 to make a pinwheel from the four half-square triangles. Press all seams open.

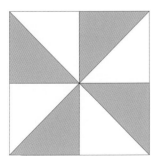

3 Glue the A paper templates to the wrong side of a scrap of light print fabric. Trim the fabric EXACTLY 1/4"

away from all sides of the templates. Turn the two, short sides of the appliqués.

Template A

4 Glue the wrong side of the appliqués in place on the pieced pinwheel block. The raw edge of the appliqués should be placed even with the raw edge of the corners of the pinwheel block.

5 Appliqué in place, leaving raw edges open. Follow directions on pages 20-21 to remove paper templates and glue. Press.

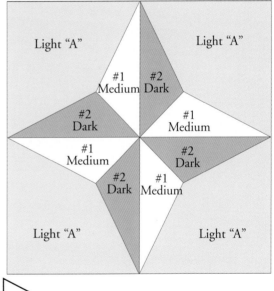

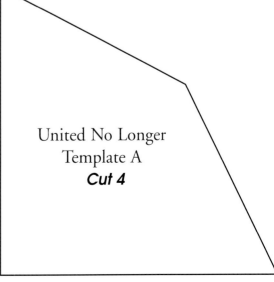

United No Longer
Template A
Cut 4

Eight-Pointed Star

Pinwheel Foundation Block

FABRICS

Light Print Fabric:
Scraps to Cut 4 of Appliqué A
& 4 of Appliqué B

Medium Print Fabric:
#1—Cut 1—4-1/2" x 8 -1/2"
Rectangle

Dark Print Fabric:
#2—Cut 1—4-1/2" x 8-1/2"
Rectangle

*Refer to General Instructions on pages 10-21
before beginning this block.*

CUTTING THE PAPER TEMPLATES

Cut four of Templates A and B.

PIECING

This block consists of 16 pieces.

1 Using Method #2, on page 50, and 3″ Triangles on a Roll™ paper, make four half-square triangles with the #1 medium print fabric and the #2 dark print fabric. Press all seams open.

2 Follow the pinwheel foundation block directions on page 56 to make a pinwheel from the four half-square triangles. Press all seams open.

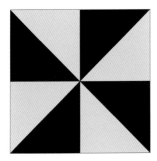

3 Glue the A and the B templates to the wrong side of a scrap of light print fabric. Trim the fabric EXACTLY 1/4" away from all sides of the templates.

Turn the two short sides of the A appliqués. Turn two adjoining sides of the B appliqués.

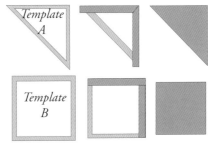

4 Glue the wrong side of the appliqués in place on the pieced pinwheel block. The raw edges of the appliqués should be placed even with the raw edges of the pinwheel block.

5 Appliqué in place, leaving raw edges open. Follow directions on pages 20-21 to remove paper templates and glue. Press.

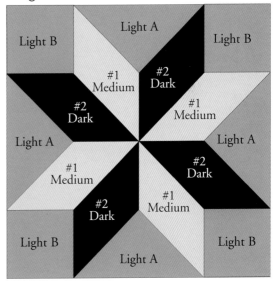

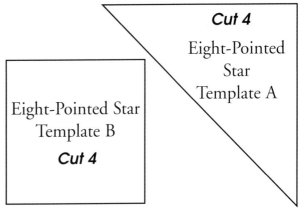

Cut 4
Eight-Pointed
Star
Template A

Eight-Pointed Star
Template B
Cut 4

Missouri Daisy

Pinwheel Foundation Block

Light Print Fabric:
Scraps to Cut 4 of Appliqué A
& 4 of Appliqué B

Medium Print Fabric:
#1—Cut 1 – 4-1/2" x 8-1/2"
Rectangle
Scrap to Cut 1 of Appliqué C

Dark Print Fabric:
#2—Cut 1 – 4-1/2" x 8-1/2"
Rectangle

*Refer to General Instructions on pages 10-21
before beginning this block.*

CUTTING THE PAPER TEMPLATES

Cut four of Templates A & B, on page 66.
Cut one of Template C, on page 66.

PIECING

This block consists of 17 pieces.

1 Using Method #2, on page 50, and 3" Triangles on a Roll™ paper, make four half-square triangles with the #1 medium print fabric and the #2 dark print fabric. Press all seams open.

2 Follow the pinwheel foundation block directions on page 56 to make a pinwheel from the four half-square triangles. Press all seams open.

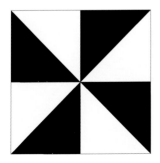

3 Glue the A and B paper templates to the wrong side of a scrap of light print fabric. Trim the fabric EXACTLY 1/4" away from all sides of the templates. Turn the two short sides of the A appliqués. Turn two adjoining sides of the B appliqués.

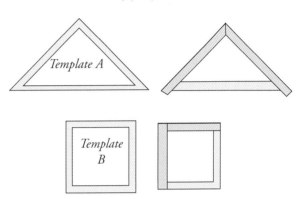

4 Glue the C paper template to the wrong side of a scrap of the medium print fabric. Trim the fabric 1/4" away from all sides of the template. Turn all sides.

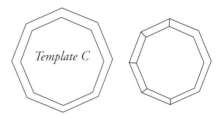

5 Glue the wrong side of the A and B appliqués in place on the pieced pinwheel block. The raw edges of the appliqués should be placed even with the raw edges of the corners of the pinwheel block. Glue the C appliqué in the center of the pinwheel.

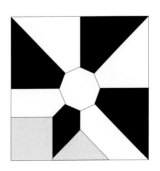

6 Appliqué in place, leaving raw edges open. Follow directions on pages 20-21 to remove paper templates and glue. Press.

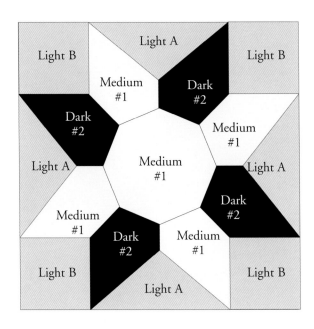

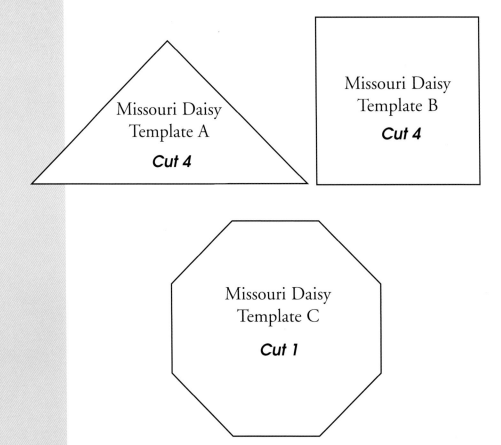

Missouri Daisy Template A

Cut 4

Missouri Daisy Template B

Cut 4

Missouri Daisy Template C

Cut 1

PLACE THE CORNER APPLIQUÉS

Glue the four corner square appliqués in place, aligning the raw edges with the raw edges of the pinwheel foundation block.

PLACE THE TRIANGLE APPLIQUÉS

Place the four triangle appliqués on the foundation block. The point of the triangle should line up with the block's seam line. Glue the wrong side of the appliqué in place.

GLUE APPLIQUÉ C

Use the glue stick on the wrong side of appliqué C.

PLACE APPLIQUÉ C

Place appliqué C on the pinwheel foundation block aligning each point with a seam line.

Kaleidoscope Foundation Block _____

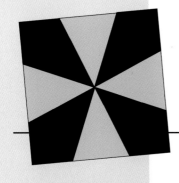

A Kaleidoscope Block is cut from a pinwheel block.

Make a sample block to learn the technique before cutting the fabric for your quilt.

FABRICS

Cut 2—6" Squares from Light Fabric

Cut 2—6" Squares from Dark Fabric

PIECING

1 Using Method #1 on page 48, make four half-square triangles from the 6" squares of light and dark fabrics. Trim these finished half-square triangles to 5".

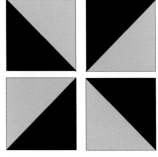

2 Sew four half-square triangles together to form a pinwheel. Press the seams open.

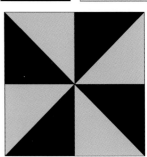

CUTTING THE KALEIDOSCOPE:

3 Glue the kaleidoscope template to the wrong side of the pinwheel block, matching the lines on the template to the seam lines of the pinwheel. The kaleidoscope block instructions state which fabric should be on the corners. Place the template accordingly.

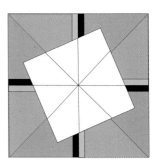

4 Place the 6-1/2" *Square it Up & Fussy Cut* Ruler on top of the template so that the 1/4" seam extends beyond the template on all sides.

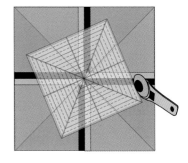

5 Cut around the ruler on all sides.

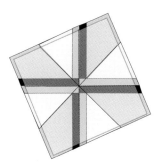

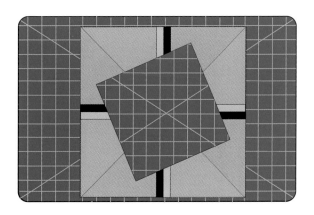

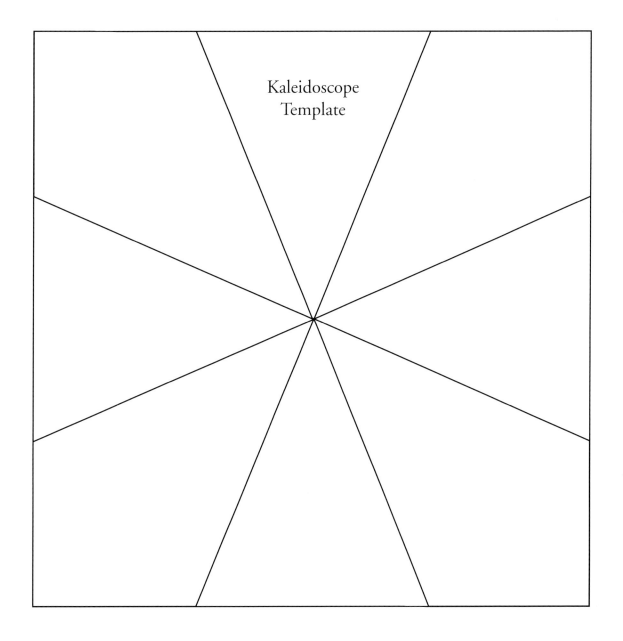

Kaleidoscope
Template

Star of the East

Kaleidoscope Foundation Block

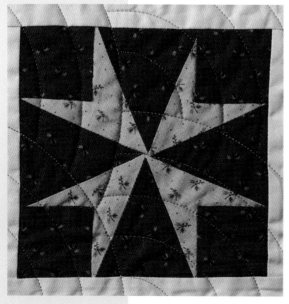

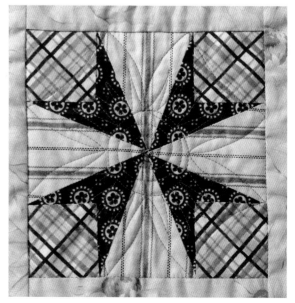

FABRICS

Medium Print Fabric:
#1—Cut 2—6" Squares

Dark Print Fabric:
#2—Cut 2—6" Squares
Scraps to Cut 4 of Appliqué A

*Refer to General Instructions on pages 10-21
before beginning this block.*

CUTTING THE PAPER TEMPLATE

Cut four of Template A.

> Star of the East
> Template A
>
> ***Cut 4***

PIECING

This block consists of 12 pieces.
Note: *Fussy cutting the appliqué
can create a dramatic block.*

1 Following the kaleidoscope
foundation block directions on
page 68, make a kaleidoscope
block with the #1 medium print
fabric squares and the #2 dark
print fabric squares. Trim the
kaleidoscope so that the medium
print fabric will form the corners of
the block.

2 Glue the A paper templates to the
wrong side of a scrap of dark print fabric.
Trim the fabric EXACTLY 1/4" away from
all sides of the templates. Turn two
adjoining sides of the A appliqués.

Template A

3 Glue the wrong side of the
appliqués in place on the pieced
kaleidoscope block. The raw edges of
the appliqués should be placed even
with the raw edges of the corners of
the kaleidoscope.

4 Appliqué in place, leaving raw edges
open. Follow directions on pages 20-21
to remove paper templates and
glue. Press.

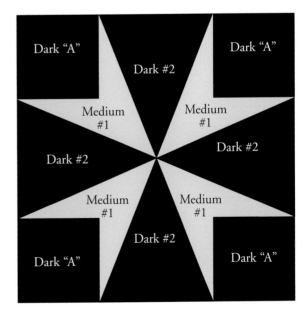

Joseph's Coat

Kaleidoscope Foundation Block

Light Print Fabric:
#1—Cut 2—6" Squares
Scraps to Cut 4 of Appliqué A

Dark Print Fabric:
#2—Cut 2—6" Squares
Scraps to Cut 4 of Appliqué B

*Refer to General Instructions on pages 10-21
before beginning this block.*

CUTTING THE PAPER TEMPLATES

Cut four of Templates A and B on page 74.

PIECING

This block consists of 16 pieces.

1 Following the kaleidoscope foundation block directions on page 68, make a kaleidoscope block with the #1 light print fabric squares and the #2 dark print fabric squares. Trim the kaleidoscope so that the dark print fabric will form the corners of the block.

2 Glue the A paper templates to the wrong side of a scrap of light print fabric. Trim the fabric EXACTLY 1/4" away from the templates on all sides. Do not turn the longest edge of the appliqué. Turn the other three sides of the A appliqués.

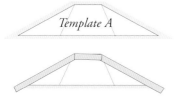

Template A

3 Glue the B paper templates to the wrong side of a scrap of dark print fabric. Trim the fabric EXACTLY 1/4" away from the templates on all sides. Turn the starred (*) sides of the templates.

Template B

4 Place the B appliqués on top of the A appliqués. Turn the top edge of the B appliqués over the A appliqués. Make a total of four of these units.

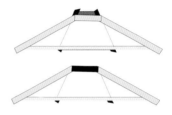

5 Glue the wrong side of the appliqués in place on the pieced kaleidoscope block. Place the long turned edges of the B appliqués on the seam lines of the kaleidoscope block. The raw edges of the appliqués should be placed even with the raw edges of the kaleidoscope block.

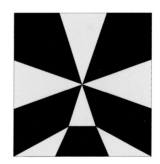

6 Appliqué in place, leaving raw edges open. Follow directions on pages 20-21 to remove paper templates and glue. Press.

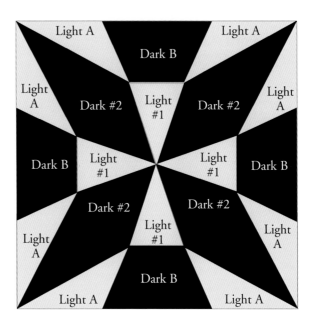

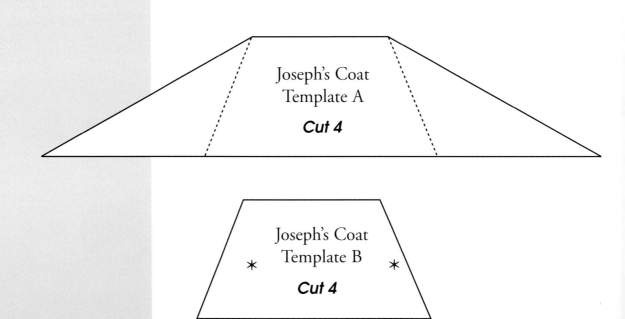

Joseph's Coat
Template A

Cut 4

Joseph's Coat
Template B

* *

Cut 4

CUT THE KALEIDOSCOPE BLOCK

Place the kaleidoscope template on the wrong side of the finished pinwheel foundation block, matching the template's lines with the block's seam lines. Lay the 6-1/2" ruler on the kaleidoscope template and cut around it.

PRESS THE FOUNDATION BLOCK

Remove the kaleidoscope template from the wrong side of the block and press. The newly formed kaleidoscope block is the foundation for Joseph's Coat.

PLACE THE LAYERED APPLIQUÉS

After gluing the wrong side of the layered appliqué, align the raw edges with the raw edges of the kaleidoscope foundation block.

FINISH THE PIECED APPLIQUÉ™ BLOCK

Continue placing the appliqués on the kaleidoscope block until the Joseph's Coat block is created. Appliqué in place, leaving raw edges open.

Quarter-Square Triangle Foundation Block

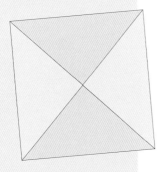

A quarter-square triangle block consists of four equal-sized triangles. It is sewn from two half-square triangles.

Note: Generally, when making quarter-square triangle blocks, the squares should be cut 1-1/4" larger than the finished block. Since you are sewing bias edges, the sewing and pressing tend to distort the shape of your finished square. I add 2" so I can square up the quarter-square triangles to the correct size after stitching and pressing.

Make a sample block to learn the technique before cutting the fabric for your quilt.

FABRICS

Cut 1—8" Square of a Light Fabric

Cut 1—8" Square of a Dark Fabric

Note: Fabric sizes given are for a quarter-square triangle sample block. Refer to your chosen block for specific fabric requirements.

PIECING

1 Make two half-square triangles with the 8" squares of light fabric and dark fabric. Press the seams open.

2 Place one half-square triangle on top of the other half-square triangle, right sides together, matching seams. The light triangle should be placed on the dark triangle.

3 Draw a diagonal line on the wrong side of the half-square triangle units. You will cross the seam line. Sew a 1/4" seam on each side of the drawn line.

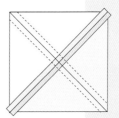

4 Cut on the drawn line. Press this final seam open. You have created two quarter-square triangles.

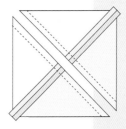

5 Place the *Square It Up & Fussy Cut* Ruler on top of the finished quarter-square triangle block, matching the diagonal lines on the ruler to the seam lines of the block. Cut around the ruler on all sides to trim the finished block to 6-1/2".

Note: In some cases, one quarter-square triangle will be used as the foundation block and will be trimmed to 6-1/2". Appliqués will be cut from the other quarter-square triangle so it should not be trimmed.

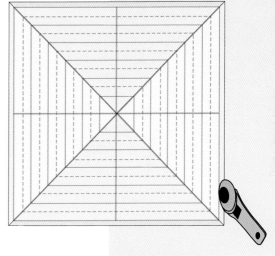

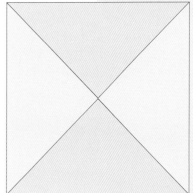

Mill and Stars

Quarter-Square Triangle Foundation Block

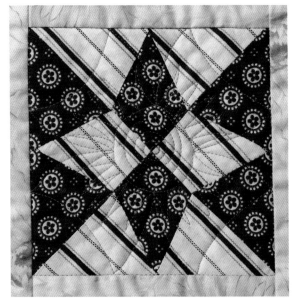

FABRICS

Light Print Fabric:
#1—Cut 1—9" Square

Medium Print Fabric:
#2—Cut 1—9" Square

Refer to General Instructions on pages 10-21 before beginning this block.

CUTTING THE PAPER TEMPLATE

Cut four of Template A.

Note: *The fabric for the A appliqués will be cut from one of the quarter-square triangle blocks.*

PIECING

This block consists of 12 pieces.

Note: *The fabrics for two of the appliqués are mirror images of the other two appliqués. Since they are cut from a completed quarter-square triangle block, they are automatically reversed for you. This also makes the finished block more stable. Only one center of a quarter-square triangle will show in the finished block, so save the "best" quarter-square triangle for the foundation block.*

1 Following the quarter-square triangle foundation block directions on page 76, make two quarter-square triangles with the #1 light print fabric square and the #2 medium print fabric square.

2 Trim one finished quarter-square triangle to 6-1/2" for the foundation block.

3 Glue the A paper templates to the wrong side of the remaining quarter-square triangle block. Match the drawn line on the template to the seam lines of the quarter-square triangle. Trim the fabric 1/4" away

from the templates on all sides. Turn the two short sides of each appliqué.

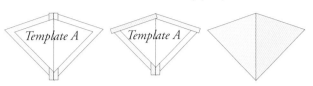

4 Glue the wrong side of the appliqués in place on the trimmed quarter-square triangle block. The raw edges of the appliqués should be placed even with the raw edges of the corner of the quarter-square triangle.

5 Appliqué in place, leaving raw edges open. Follow directions on pages 20-21 to remove paper templates and glue. Press.

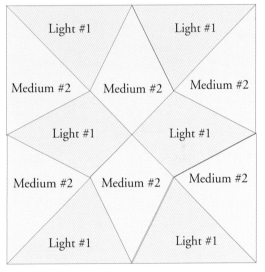

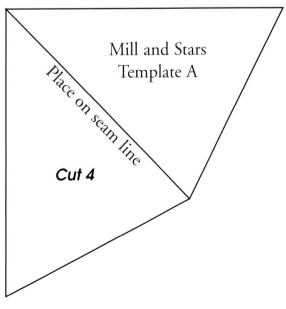

Mill and Stars
Template A

Place on seam line

Cut 4

The Arrow Star

Quarter-Square Triangle Foundation Block

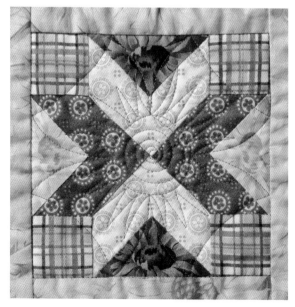

Light Print Fabric:
Scraps to Cut 4 of Appliqué A
& 4 of Appliqué B

Medium Print Fabric:
#1—Cut 1—8" Square

Dark Print Fabric:
#2—Cut 1—8" Square

*Refer to General Instructions on pages 10-21
before beginning this block.*

CUTTING THE PAPER TEMPLATES

Cut four of Templates A and B.

PIECING

This block consists of 12 pieces.

1 Following the quarter-square triangle foundation block directions on page 76, make two quarter-square triangles with the #1 medium print fabric square and the #2 dark print fabric square. You will only need one, so choose the block that has the best center seam match. The other block is extra.

2 Trim one finished quarter-square triangle to 6-1/2".

3 Glue the A and the B paper templates to the wrong side of the scrap of light print fabric. Trim the fabric 1/4" away from the templates on all sides. Turn the two short sides of the A appliqués. Turn two adjoining sides of the B appliqués.

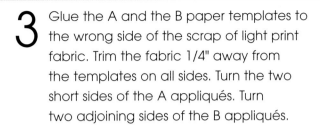

Template A

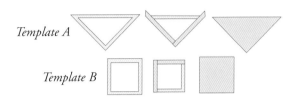

Template B

4 Glue the wrong side of the appliqués in place on the trimmed quarter-square triangle block. The raw edges of the appliqués should be placed even with the raw edges of the quarter-square triangle block.

5 Appliqué in place, leaving raw edges open. Follow directions on pages 20-21 to remove paper templates and glue. Press.

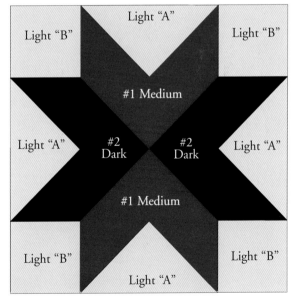

Light "A" · Light "B" · Light "B" · #1 Medium · Light "A" · #2 Dark · #2 Dark · Light "A" · #1 Medium · Light "B" · Light "B" · Light "A"

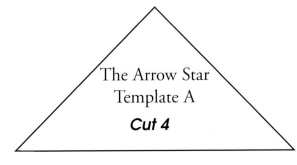

The Arrow Star
Template A
Cut 4

The Arrow Star
Template B
Cut 4

Jeri's Star

Nine-Patch Foundation Block

Light Print Fabric:
#1—Cut 4—2" Squares
Scraps to Cut 4 of Appliqué A

Medium Print Fabric:
#2—Cut 1—3-1/2" Square

Dark Print Fabric:
#3—Cut 4—2" x 3-1/2" Rectangles

*Refer to General Instructions on pages 10-21
before beginning this block.*

CUTTING THE PAPER TEMPLATE

Cut four of Template A.

PIECING

This block consists of 13 pieces.
> **Note:** *The center 3-1/2" cut square
> is a great place to fussy cut a
> beautiful fabric.*

1 Following the nine-patch foundation
block directions on page 40, make
a nine-patch with the #2 medium
print square (center); the #1 light
print squares (corners); and the #3
dark print rectangles. Press the
seams open.

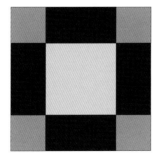

2 Glue the A paper templates to the
wrong side of a scrap of light print
fabric. Place the longest side of
the A templates on the straight of
grain. Trim the fabric 1/4" away
from the templates on all sides.

Turn the two short sides. Do not turn the
longest side.

3 Glue the wrong side of the appliqués
in place on the pieced foundation
block. The raw edges of the appliqués
should be placed even with the raw
edges of the pieced block.

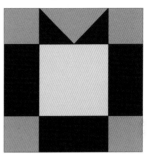

4 Appliqué in place, leaving raw edges
open. Follow directions on pages 20-21
to remove paper templates and
glue. Press.

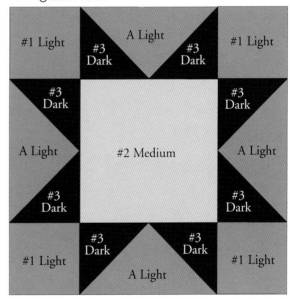

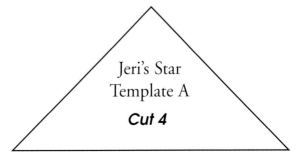

Jeri's Star
Template A

Cut 4

TRIM THE FOUNDATION BLOCK

Trim the finished quarter-square triangle foundation block to 6-1/2". Refer to page 76 to make a quarter-square triangle foundation block.

GLUE THE APPLIQUÉS IN PLACE

Place the square appliqués, glue side down on the foundation block's corners. Align the unfinished edges of the appliqués with the raw edges of the block.

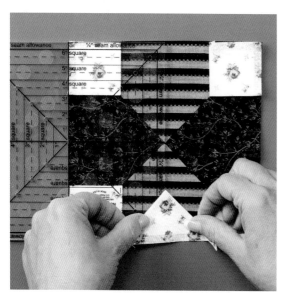

ALIGN THE TRIANGLE APPLIQUÉS

Align the center point of the triangle appliqué with the center point of the foundation block by placing a ruler's edge where the quarter-square triangles meet.

PLACE THE REMAINING APPLIQUÉS

Place the remaining triangle appliqués on the foundation block. Trim the tails and stitch the appliqués in place, leaving the raw edges open. Remove templates and glue, referring to pages 20-21.

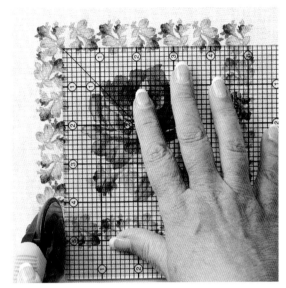

FUSSY CUT THE FABRIC

Fussy cut a beautiful fabric or motif
for the center square of your nine-patch
foundation block.

SEW THE FOUNDATION BLOCK

Build the rest of your nine-patch foundation
block around your fussy cut center square

PLACE THE APPLIQUÉS

Align the raw edges of the triangle
appliqués with the unfinished edges
of the nine-patch foundation block.
Glue in place.

FINISH THE BLOCK

Continue gluing the triangle appliqués
in place; turning the foundation block
as you go. Stitch the glued appliqués in
place, leaving raw edges open. Remove
templates and glue, following directions on
pages 20-21.

St. Gregory's Cross

Nine-Patch Foundation Block

Light Print Fabric:
#1—Cut 1—2 -1/2" Square
Scraps to cut 4 of Appliqué A

Medium Light Print Fabric:
Scraps to cut 4 of Appliqué B

Medium Print Fabric:
#2—Cut 4—2-1/2" Squares

Dark Print Fabric:
#3—Cut 4—2-1/2" Squares

*Refer to General Instructions on pages 10-21
before beginning this block.*

CUTTING THE PAPER TEMPLATES

Cut four of Templates A and B on page 88.

PIECING

This block consists of 17 pieces.
Note: *Try fussy cutting the center light print 2-1/2" square and the A appliqués.*

1 Following the nine-patch foundation block directions on page 40, make a nine-patch with the #1 light print square (center); the #3 dark print squares (corners); and the #2 medium print squares. Press the seams open.

2 Glue the A paper templates to the wrong side of a scrap of light print fabric. Trim the fabric EXACTLY 1/4" away from all sides of the templates.

Turn two opposite sides of each appliqué. Do not turn the other two sides.

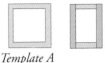

Template A

3 Glue the wrong side of the appliqués in place on the pieced nine-patch block. The raw edges of the appliqués will be covered by the B appliqués.

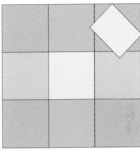

4 Glue the B paper templates to the wrong side of a scrap of medium light print fabric. Trim the fabric EXACTLY 1/4" away from all sides of the templates. Turn the two sides that form right triangles. Do not turn the two short, straight sides.

Template B

5 Glue the wrong side of the appliqués in place on the pieced block. Place the raw edges of the appliqués even with the raw edges of the pieced block.

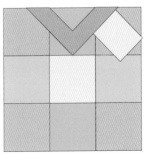

6 Appliqué in place, leaving raw edges open. Follow directions on pages 20-21 to remove paper templates and glue. Press.

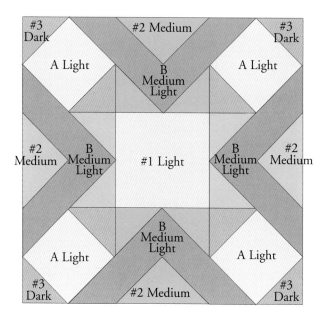

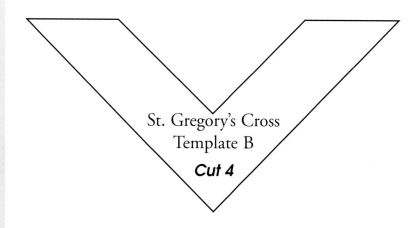

St. Gregory's Cross
Template A

Cut 4

St. Gregory's Cross
Template B

Cut 4

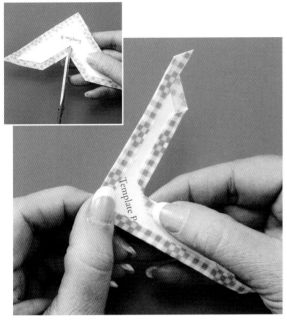

CLIP AND TURN FABRIC

To create a smooth line when turning an inside corner, take a small scissors and clip the fabric to within a few threads of the template. Run a glue stick along the template's edge and turn the fabric.

GLUE THE APPLIQUÉS

Glue the wrong side of the A appliqués in place on the nine-patch foundation block. The raw edges of the A appliqués will be covered by the B appliqués.

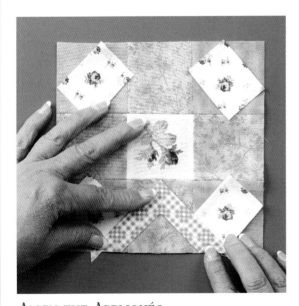

ALIGN THE APPLIQUÉS

Glue the the B appliqués to the foundation block. Place the raw edges of the appliqués even with the raw edges of the pieced block.

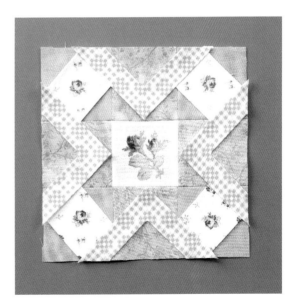

TRIM THE APPLIQUÉS

Trim the tails of the appliqués even with the pieced foundation block. Stitch in place. leaving raw edges open.

Sarah's Choice

Nine-Patch Foundation Block

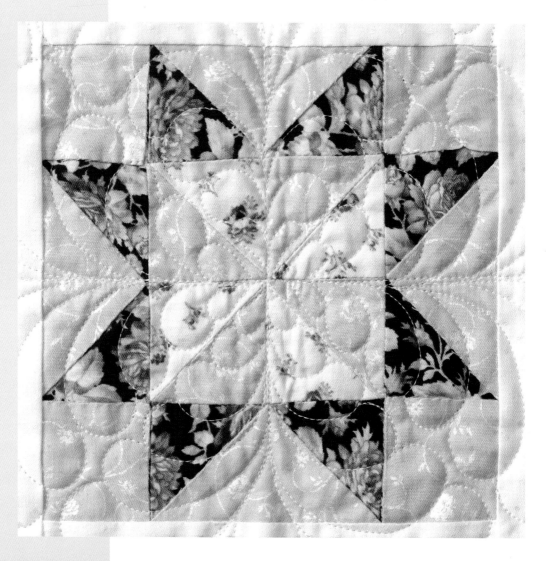

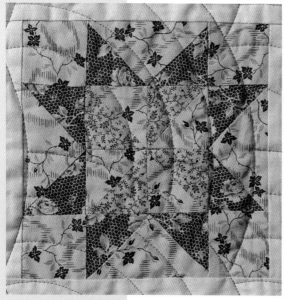

FABRICS

Light Print Fabric:
#1—Cut 2—3" Squares

Medium Print Fabric:
#2—Cut 2—3" Squares
#3—Cut 4—2" Squares
Scraps to Cut 4 of Appliqué A

Dark Print Fabric:
#4—Cut 4—2" x 3-1/2" Rectangles

*Refer to General Instructions on pages 10-21
before beginning this block.*

CUTTING THE PAPER TEMPLATE

Cut four of Template A.

PIECING

This block consists of 20 pieces.

1 Using Method #1 on page 48, make four half-square triangles with the #1 light print fabric and the #2 medium print fabric. Trim these half-square triangles to 2".

2 Following the pinwheel block directions on page 56, make a pinwheel from the four half-square triangles. This pinwheel is the center square of the nine-patch block.

3 Following the nine-patch foundation block directions on page 40, make a nine-patch with the pinwheel (center); the #3 medium print squares (corners); and the #4 dark print rectangles. Press the seams open.

4 Glue the A paper templates to the wrong side of a scrap of light print fabric. Place the longest edge of the A paper templates on the straight of grain. Trim the fabric EXACTLY 1/4" away from the templates on all sides. Turn the two, short sides.

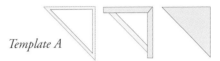

Template A

5 Glue the wrong side of the appliqués in place on the pieced block. The raw edges of the appliqués should be placed even with the raw edges of the pieced block.

6 Appliqué in place, leaving raw edges open. Follow directions on pages 20-21 to remove paper templates and glue. Press.

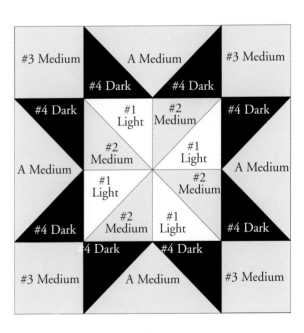

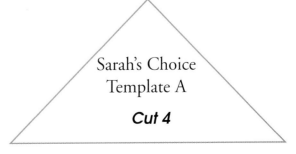

Sarah's Choice
Template A

Cut 4

Set on Point Foundation Block

When a block or quilt is set on point, it is turned 90 degrees. In the block, Debby's Nine-Patch Art, on page 94, a nine-patch is placed on point by sewing triangles to opposite sides of the center square.

Make a sample block to learn the technique before cutting the fabric for your quilt.

FABRICS

Light Print: #1
Cut 2—4-1/2" Squares

Cut once on the Diagonal

Medium Print: #2
Cut 4—1-7/8" Squares

Dark Print: #3
Cut 5—1-7/8" Squares

PIECING

1   Following the nine-patch block directions on page 40, make a nine-patch from the #2 medium print squares and the #3 dark print squares. Press all seams open.

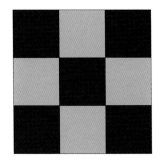

2   Center and sew a light print triangle to opposite sides of the nine-patch. Press the seams open.

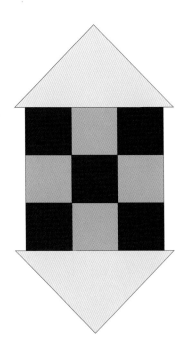

3 Trim off the points of the triangle even with the sides of the nine-patch.

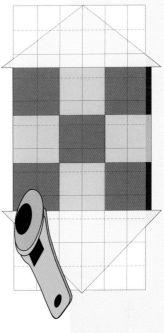

4 Center and sew a light print triangle to the remaining two sides of the nine-patch. Press the seams open.

5 Place the *Square It Up & Fussy Cut* Ruler on the block so that the horizontal and vertical lines on the ruler intersect the points of the nine-patch.

6 Trim all four sides.

Debby's Nine-Patch Art

Set on Point Foundation Block

Light Print Fabric:
#1—Cut 2—4-1/2" Squares
Cut once on the Diagonal

Medium Print Fabric:
#2—Cut 4—1-7/8" Squares

Dark Print Fabric:
#3—Cut 5—1-7/8" Squares
Scraps to Cut 4 of Appliqué A

*Refer to General Instructions on pages 10-21
before beginning this block.*

CUTTING THE PAPER TEMPLATE

Cut four of Template A.

Debby's
Nine-Patch Art
Template A

Cut 4

PIECING

This block consists of 17 pieces.

1 Following the nine-patch block directions on page 40, make a nine-patch from the #2 medium print squares and the #3 dark print squares. Press all seams open.

2 Referring to the set on point foundation block directions on page 92, center and sew a #1 light print triangle to opposite sides of the nine-patch. Press the seams open. The triangles will be over-sized. Trim the points of the triangles even with the center square.

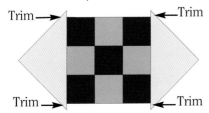

3 Center and sew the remaining #1 light print triangles to the other two sides of the unit pieced in Step #2. Press the seams open. The triangles will be over-sized.

4 Trim this pieced block to 6-1/2". Each side should measure 3-1/4" from the center point.

5 Glue the A paper templates to the wrong side of a scrap of dark print fabric. Trim the fabric EXACTLY 1/4" away from the templates on all sides. Turn two adjoining sides of the A appliqués.

Template A

6 Glue the wrong side of the appliqués in place on the pieced block. The raw edges of the appliqués should be placed even with the raw edges of the pieced block.

7 Appliqué in place, leaving raw edges open. Follow directions on pages 20-21 to remove paper templates and glue. Press.

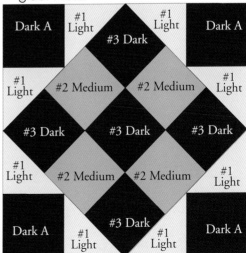

Boston Uncommon

Set on Point Foundation Block

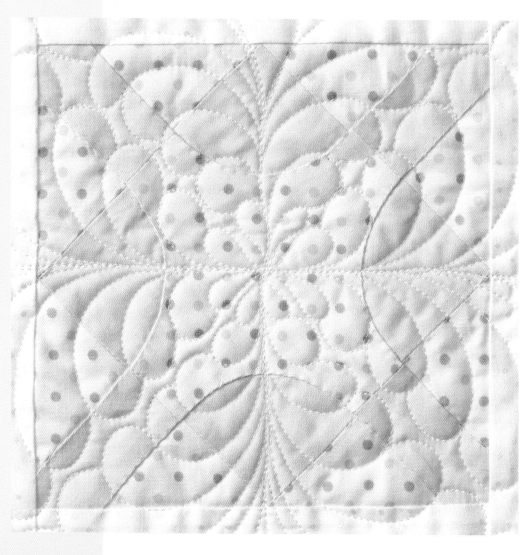

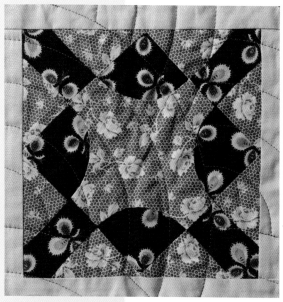

Light Print Fabric:
#1—Cut 1—4-3/4" Square
#2—Cut 2—4-1/2" Squares
Cut once on the Diagonal

Medium Print Fabric:
#3—Cut 1—4-3/4" Square
#4—Cut 2—4-1/2" Squares
Cut once on the Diagonal

*Refer to General Instructions on pages 10-21
before beginning this block.*

CUTTING THE PAPER TEMPLATE

Cut one of Template A on page 98.

PIECING

This block consists of 10 pieces.
   Note: *The fabric for the A appliqué will be cut from the pieced block with the light print center square.*

1 Referring to the set on point foundation block directions on page 92, center and sew the longest edge of a #2 light print triangle to opposite sides of the #3 medium print square. Press the seams open. The triangles will be over-sized. Trim the points of the triangles even with the center square.

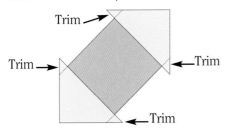

2 Center and sew the remaining #2 light print triangles to the other two sides of the unit completed in Step #1. Press the seams open. The triangles will be over-sized. Press seams open.

3 Trim this pieced block to 6-1/2". Each side should measure 3-1/4" from the center point.

4 Repeat steps 1 - 3 using the #4 medium print triangles and the #1 light print square.

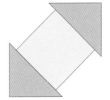

5 Glue the wrong side of the A paper template to the wrong side of the block completed in Step 4, matching the drawn lines on the template to the seam lines on the pieced block. Trim the fabric 1/4" away from all of the curved edges and turn. Trim the straight edges 1/4" away from the template. Do not turn the straight edges.

Template A

6 Glue the wrong side of the appliqué in place on the remaining pieced Set on Point foundation block, matching the seam lines on the appliqué to the seam lines on the pieced block. The raw edges of the appliqués should be placed even with the raw edges of the outside edge of the remaining pieced block.

7 Appliqué in place, leaving raw edges open. Follow directions on pages 20-21 to remove paper templates and glue. Press.

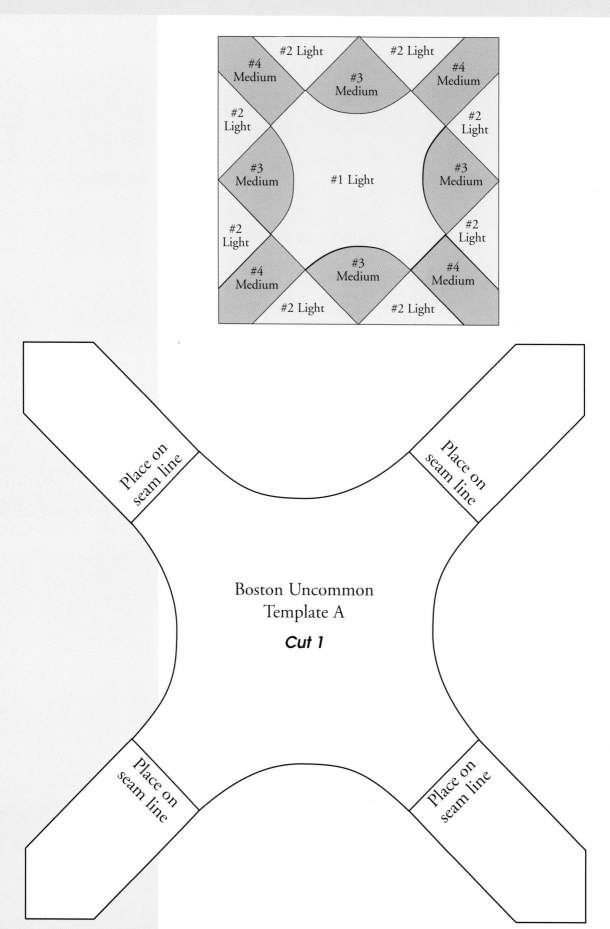

Boston Uncommon
Template A

Cut 1

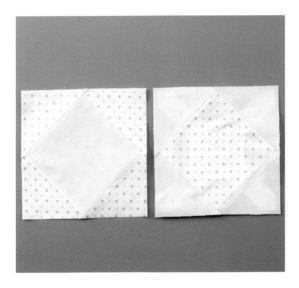

MAKE TWO BLOCKS

The Boston Uncommon block requires two set on point foundation blocks. The blocks should be a mirror image of each other.

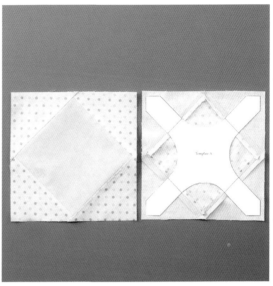

MATCH LINES

Glue the wrong side of the paper template to the back of one of the set on point blocks. Match the drawn lines on the paper template to the seam lines on the block.

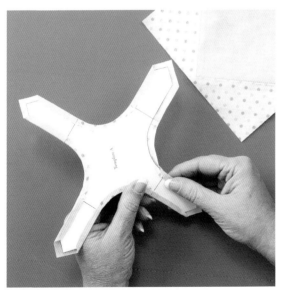

TURN THE FABRIC

Turn the fabric to the wrong side of the paper template. Since this is a gentle curve the fabric should turn easily without any clipping.

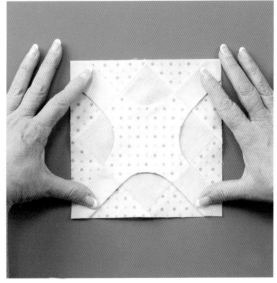

PLACE THE APPLIQUÉ

Glue the wrong side of the appliqué in place on the remaining pieced block, matching the seam lines on the appliqué to the seam lines on the pieced block.

Sue's Hot Cross Buns

6" Foundation Block

Light Print Fabric:
#1—Cut 1—6-1/2" Square
Scraps to Cut 2 of Appliqué C

Medium Print Fabric:
Scraps to Cut 2 of Appliqué B

Dark Print Fabric:
Scraps to Cut 2 of Appliqué A

*Refer to General Instructions on pages 10-21
before beginning this block.*
See Tip on page 103 before beginning.

CUTTING THE PAPER TEMPLATES

Cut two of Templates A, B, and C on pages 102 and 103.

PIECING

This block consists of 7 pieces.

1 Glue the A paper templates to the wrong side of a scrap of the dark print fabric. Trim the fabric 1/4" away from the templates on all sides. Turn the two long sides of each appliqué.

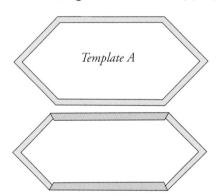

Template A

2 Glue the B paper templates to the wrong side of a scrap of the medium print fabric. Trim the fabric 1/4" away from the templates on all sides. Turn the two long sides of each appliqué.

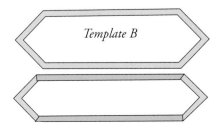

Template B

3 Glue the C paper templates to the wrong side of a scrap of the light print fabric. Trim the fabric 1/4" away from the templates on all sides. Turn the two long sides of each appliqué.

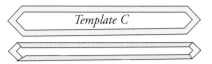

Template C

4 Center and diagonally place the A appliqués on the #1 light print square. Stitch in place. Remove the paper templates and press. See page 103.

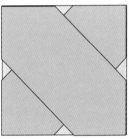

5 Center and diagonally place the B appliqués on the top of the A appliqués. Stitch in place. Remove the paper templates and press. See page 103.

6 Center and diagonally place the C appliqués on the top of the B appliqués. Stitch in place. Remove the paper templates and press. See page 103.

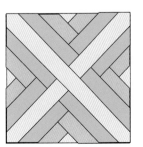

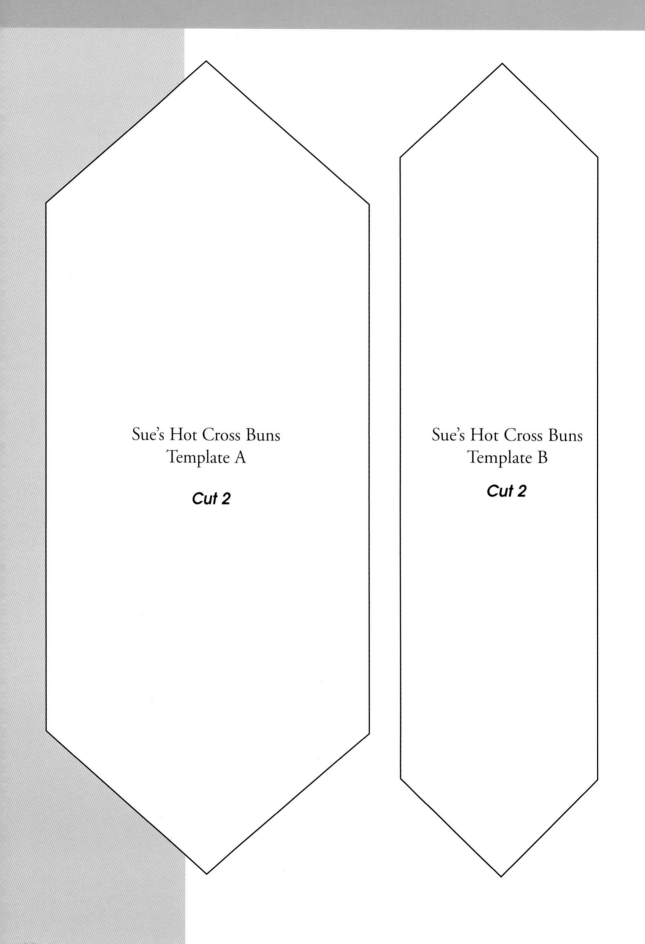

Sue's Hot Cross Buns
Template A

Cut 2

Sue's Hot Cross Buns
Template B

Cut 2

Sue's
Hot
Cross
Buns
Template
C

Cut 2

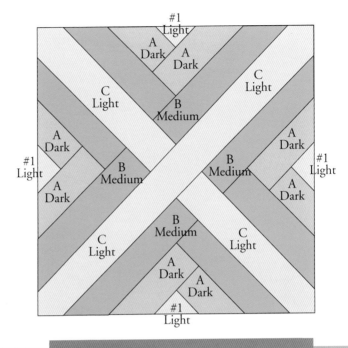

TIP

Method 1: *Stitch each appliqué, one at a time, to the foundation block, leaving the raw edges open. Remove the paper templates and glue of each appliqué before adding the next. Sue's Hot Cross Buns instructions on page 101 uses Method 1.*

Method 2: *You may layer your appliqué pieces and glue them to the foundation block all at one time. If you choose this method, be sure to stitch each appliqué only to the fabric directly below, leaving the raw edges open. Do not go clear down to the foundation block. You don't want to sew the templates into your work.*

Removing Paper Templates & Glue: *To remove paper templates and glue, soak the appliquéd block in warm water for at least twenty minutes. Roll it in a towel to remove the excess water. Smooth it out and let it dry. Pull out the paper templates. If using Method 2, slit or cut the background fabric to remove any inside templates. Run the seams under water to flush out any remaining glue.*

Keri's Star

6" Foundation Block

FABRICS

Light Print Fabric:
Scraps to Cut 4 of Appliqué A

Medium Print Fabric:
#1—Cut 1—6-1/2" Square
#2—Cut 1—2" Square

Dark Print Fabric:
#3—Cut 2—2" x 2-3/4" Rectangles
Scrap to Cut 1 of Appliqué B

*Refer to General Instructions on pages 10-21
before beginning this block.*

CUTTING THE PAPER TEMPLATES

Cut four of Template A, one of Template
B, and one of Template C on page 107.

PIECING

This block consists of 9 pieces.
Note: *The fabric for Appliqué C is
cut from a pieced unit.*

1 Glue the A paper templates to the
wrong side of a scrap of light print
fabric. Place the longest side of the
template on the straight of grain. Trim
the fabric EXACTLY 1/4" away from
the templates on all sides. Turn the
two short sides of each appliqué.

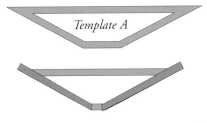

Template A

2 Glue the wrong side of the appliqués
in place on the #1 medium print
square. The raw edge of the

appliqué should be placed even with the
raw edge of the square.

3 Glue the B paper template to the wrong
side of a scrap of dark print fabric. Trim
the fabric 1/4" away from the template
on all sides. Turn the two long sides of
the appliqué.

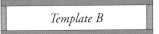

Template B

4 Center and glue the wrong side of
the appliqué in place on the block
completed in Step 2.

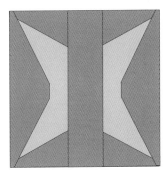

5 Sew a #3 dark print rectangle to opposite
sides of the #2 medium print square. Press
the seams open.

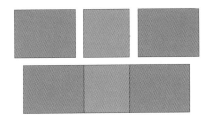

6 Glue the C paper template to the wrong side of the unit pieced in Step #5. Match the seam lines to the drawn lines on the template. Turn the two long sides of the appliqué.

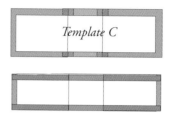

Template C

7 Center and glue the wrong side of the C appliqué in place on the block completed in Step #4. Match the seam lines to the sides of the B appliqué.

8 Appliqué in place, leaving raw edges open. Follow directions on pages 20-21 to remove paper templates and glue. Press.

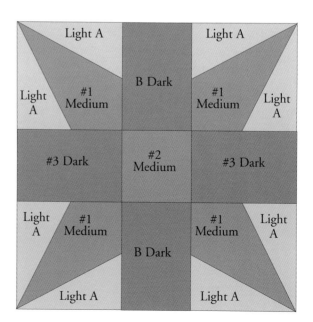

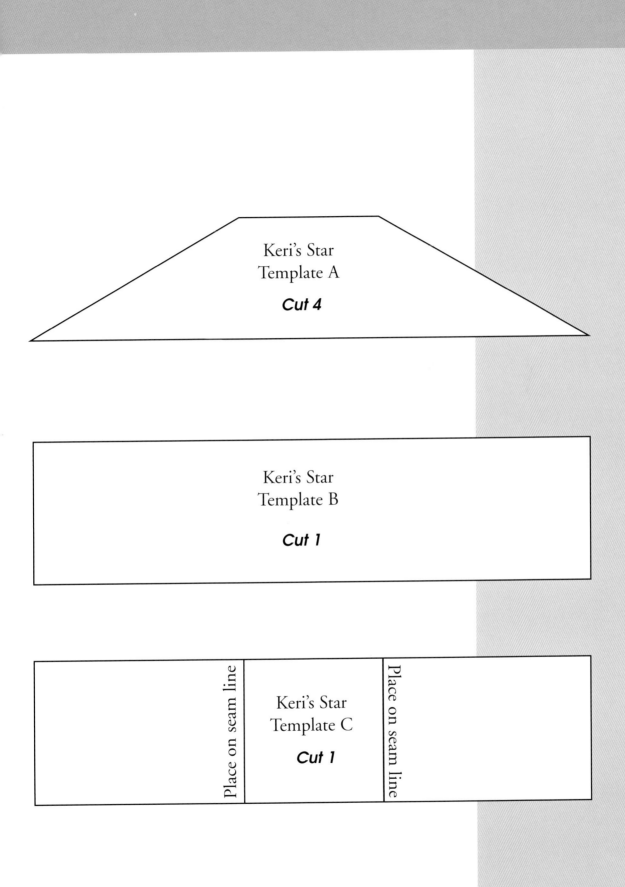

Keri's Star
Template A

Cut 4

Keri's Star
Template B

Cut 1

Place on seam line

Keri's Star
Template C

Cut 1

Place on seam line

Bright Hopes Foundation Block

A Bright Hopes block consists of a center square surrounded by four rectangles of equal size. This method eliminates the need to sew an inset point.

Make a sample block to learn the technique before cutting the fabric for your quilt.

FABRICS

4—2-1/2" x 4-1/2"
Rectangles

1—2-1/2" Square for
the Center Square

Note: Fabric sizes
given are for a
Bright Hopes sample
block. Refer to your
chosen block for specific
fabric requirements.

PIECING

1 Lay the center square, right sides together on one of the rectangles. Sew a partial seam approximately 1- 3/4" long. Press the seam open.

2 Place the seamed edge, right sides together, on a 2-1/2" x 4-1/2" rectangle of fabric. Sew along the 4-1/2" length. Press the seam open.

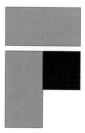

3 Place the seamed edge, right sides together, on a 2-1/2" x 4-1/2" rectangle of fabric. Sew along the 4-1/2" length. Press the seam open.

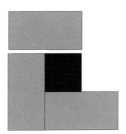

4 Place the seamed edge, right sides together, on a 2-1/2" x 4-1/2" rectangle of fabric. Sew along the 4-1/2" length. Press the seam open.

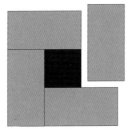

5 Finish sewing the partial seam to connect the first 2-1/2" x 4-1/2" rectangle. Press the seam open.

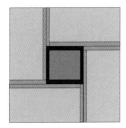 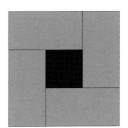

Whirligigs

Bright Hopes Foundation Block

Light Print Fabric:
Scraps to Cut 4 of Appliqué A

Medium Print Fabric:
#1—Cut 1—3-1/2" Square

Dark Print Fabric:
#2—Cut 4—2" x 5" Rectangles

*Refer to General Instructions on pages 10-21
before beginning this block.*

CUTTING THE PAPER TEMPLATE

Cut four of Template A.

PIECING

This block consists of 9 pieces.
Note: *Try fussy cutting the
center square.*

1 Following the Bright Hopes
foundation block directions on
page 108, piece a Bright Hopes
block from the #1 medium print
square and the #2 dark print
rectangles. Press the seams toward
the dark print rectangles.

2 Glue the A paper templates to the
wrong side of a scrap of the light print
fabric. Trim the fabric 1/4" away from
the templates on all sides. Turn the
two short sides of each appliqué.

Template A

3 Glue the wrong side of the A appliqués
in place on the pieced Bright Hopes
block. The raw edge of the appliqués
should be placed even with the raw
edges of the Bright Hopes block.

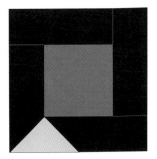

4 Appliqué in place, leaving raw edges
open. Follow directions on pages 20-21
to remove paper templates and
glue. Press.

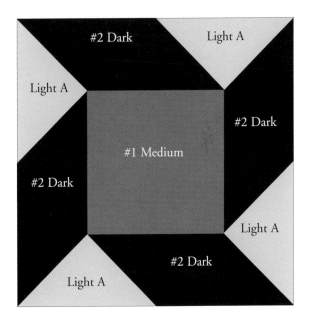

#2 Dark — Light A — Light A — #2 Dark — #1 Medium — #2 Dark — Light A — #2 Dark — Light A

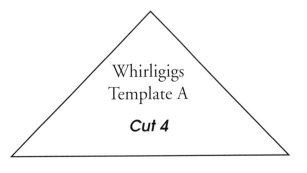

Whirligigs
Template A

Cut 4

Windblown Square

Bright Hopes Foundation Block

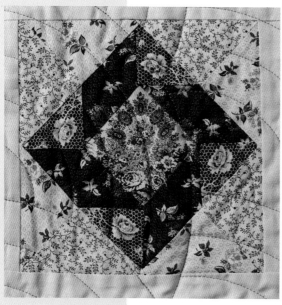

Light Print Fabric:
#1—Cut 1—4-1/2" Square
Sub-cut Both Ways
on the Diagonal

Medium Light Print Fabric:
#2—Cut 1—4-1/2" Square
Sub-cut Both Ways
on the Diagonal

Fussy Cut Center:
#3—Cut 1—2-1/2" Square

Medium Print Fabric:
Scraps to Cut 4 of Appliqué A

Dark Print Fabric:
#4—Cut 4—1-5/8" x 3-7/8"
Rectangles

*Refer to General Instructions on pages 10-21
before beginning this block.*

CUTTING THE PAPER TEMPLATE

Cut four of Template A on page 114.

PIECING

This block consists of 17 pieces.

1 Following the Bright Hopes foundation block directions on page 108, piece a Bright Hopes block from the #3 fussy cut center and the #4 dark print rectangles. Press the seams toward the dark print rectangles.

2 Glue the A paper templates to the wrong side of a scrap of the medium print fabric. Trim the fabric 1/4" away from the template on all sides. Turn the two short sides of each appliqué.

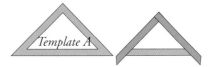

Template A

3 Glue the wrong side of the A appliqués in place on the pieced Bright Hopes block. The raw edge of the appliqués should be placed even with the raw edges of the Bright Hopes block.

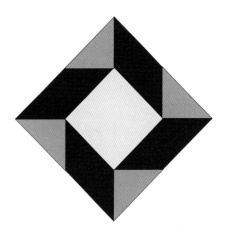

4 Appliqué in place, leaving raw edges open. Follow directions on pages 20-21 to remove paper templates and glue. Press.

5 Sew a #1 light print triangle to a #2 medium light print triangle along one of the short sides. Press the seam open. Make a total of four identical units.

113

6 Center and sew the units pieced in Step #5 to opposite sides of the Bright Hopes block. Press the seams toward the triangle units. These units are over-sized. Trim the points of the triangles even with the Bright Hopes block.

7 Center and sew the remaining units pieced in Step #5 to the other two sides of the Bright Hopes block. Press the seams toward the triangle units. These units are over-sized.

8 Trim the finished block to 6-1/2" - 1/4" beyond the corners of the Bright Hopes block (see photo on page 115).

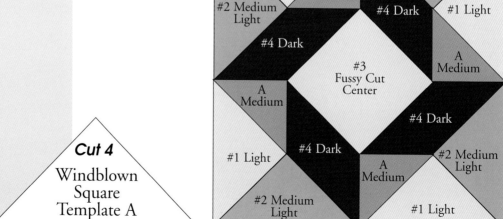

PLACE THE APPLIQUÉS

Glue the wrong side of the appliqués in place on the Bright Hopes foundation block. The raw edge of the appliqué should be placed even with the raw edge of the block. Appliqué in place, leaving raw edges open. Remove the paper templates and press.

SEW THE TRIANGLE UNITS

Center and sew the triangle units to opposite sides of the Bright Hopes foundation block. The units are over-sized.

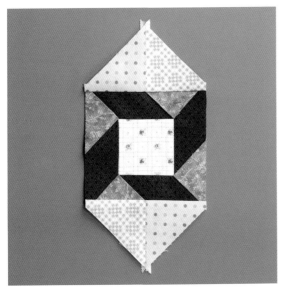

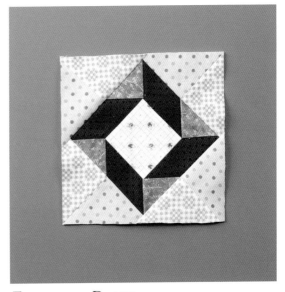

TRIM THE TRIANGLE POINTS

Trim the points of the over-sized triangle units even with the Bright Hopes block.

FINISH THE BLOCK

Sew the two remaining triangle units to the foundation block. Trim to 6-1/2".

Designing
the Quilt

Cottage Charm Quilt

LaBelle Rose by Holly Holderman for LakeHouse Dry Goods

Quilt pieced by Jan Creekmore; quilted by Cheryl Lorence

Block placement from left to right

Row 1	Whirligigs	Joseph's Coat	Boston Uncommon	
Row 2	Old Windmills	Missouri Daisy	Eight-Pointed Star	Debby's Nine-Patch Art
Row 3	Kitty's World	1941 Star	Attic Windows	
Row 4	Keri's Star	Sue's Hot Cross Buns	Mill & Stars	Bow Tie
Row 5	King David's Crown	Jeri's Star	The Arrow Star	
Row 6	Lover's Knot	Star of the East	United No Longer	Hummingbird
Row 7	Grandmother's Choice	Sarah's Choice	Windblown Square	

Bound for Glory Quilt

New Nation from Windham Fabrics by Nancy Gere for Windham Fabrics

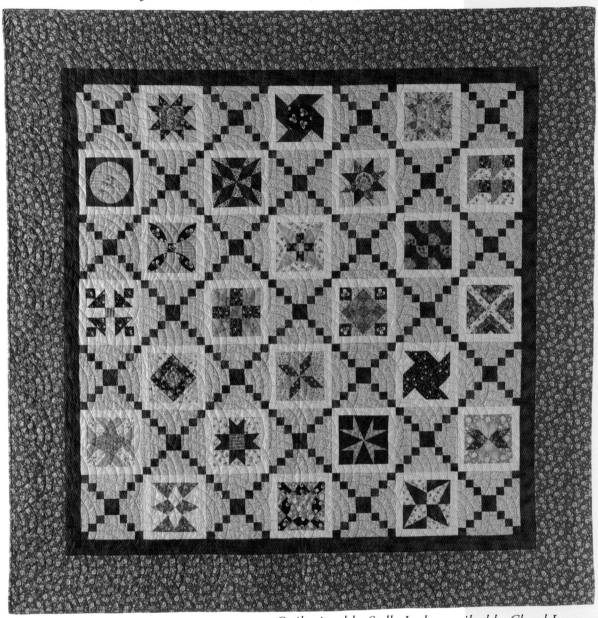

Quilt pieced by Stella Jordan; quilted by Cheryl Lorence

Block placement from left to right

Row 1	Jeri's Star	Whirligigs	Sarah's Choice	
Row 2	Kitty's World	Joseph's Coat	Missouri Daisy	Attic Windows
Row 3	Lover's Knot	King David's Crown	Bow Tie	
Row 4	Grandmother's Choice	Keri's Star	Debby's Nine-Patch Art	Sue's Hot Cross Buns
Row 5	Windblown Square	Eight-Pointed Star	Old Windmills	
Row 6	United No Longer	1941 Star	Star of the East	The Arrow Star
Row 7	Mill & Stars	Boston Uncommon	Hummingbird	

Sunflower Surround Quilt

Full Sun designed by WillowBerry Lane for Maywood Fabrics

Quilt pieced by Jeannie Downey; quilted by Cheryl Lorence

Block placement from left to right

Row 1	Old Windmills	1941 Star	Attic Windows	
Row 2	United No Longer	Lover's Knot	Jeri's Star	Grandmother's Choice
Row 3	Whirligigs	Joseph's Coat	Eight-Pointed Star	
Row 4	Kitty's World	The Arrow Star	Boston Uncommon	Keri's Star
Row 5	Sue's Hot Cross Buns	King David's Crown	Missouri Daisy	
Row 6	Windblown Square	Hummingbird	St. Gregory's Cross	Debby's Nine-Patch Art
Row 7	Bow Tie	Star of the East	Mill & Stars	

If you love...

the easy-to-create blocks in this book,
you're in luck, more blocks are on the way.
Watch for new books, blocks, and projects by
Penny using her innovative Pieced Appliqué™
techniques. Blocks from this book and future
books are featured in the quilt below.

Quilt pieced by Rose Wetherill; quilted by Nada Garvin

The Quilt

Now that you've discovered the simplicity of creating Pieced Appliqué™ blocks, it's time to combine them into a stunning display.

The quilt shown is made with twenty-four of the Pieced Appliqué™ blocks. Use the twenty-fifth block as a label on the back of your quilt. Arrange your blocks in a way that pleases you, the photo below is only a reference. Be creative.

74" Square

FABRICS

Light Print Fabric
1-1/2 yards for sashing for the
Pieced Appliqué™ blocks

Medium Pink Print Fabric
2 yards for the
Pieced Setting blocks

Dark Print Fabric
1 yard for the squares in the
Pieced Setting blocks

Green Print Fabric
1/2 yard for the Inner Border

Floral Print Fabric
2-1/8 yards for the Outer
Border and Binding

Backing Fabric
5 yards

Light Print Fabric:
#1—Cut 3—6-1/2" strips
Sub-cut each strip into
16—2-1/2" x 6-1/2" strips
for a total of 48 strips

#2—Cut 3—10-1/2" strips
Sub-cut each strip into
16—2-1/2" x 10-1/2" strips
for a total of 48 strips

**Make 24 Pieced Appliqué™
Blocks with sashing**

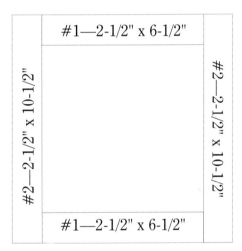

PIECING:

1 Sew a 2-1/2" x 6-1/2" light print strip to opposite sides of the Pieced Appliqué™ block. Press the seams toward the light print strips.

2 Sew a 2-1/2" x 10-1/2" light print strip to the each remaining side. Press the seams toward the light print strips.

Note: These squares have a built in "fudge actor". If the Pieced Appliqué™ block is not exactly 6-1/2", trim the sashing strips to the width of the block. After the sashings are added, place the 8-1/2" Square It Up & Fussy Cut ruler on each Pieced Appliqué™ block. The diagonal lines on the ruler should intersect the corners of the block. Trim all sides of the sashed Pieced Appliqué™ block.

CUTTING
PIECED SETTING BLOCKS

Medium Pink Print Fabric:

#2—Cut 4—1-1/2" strips

#3—Cut 2—2-1/2" strips

#4—Cut 4—4-1/2" strips
Sub-cut two strips into
26—1-1/2" x 4-1/2"
rectangles

#5—Cut 6—6-1/2" strips
Sub-cut three strips into
26—2" x 6-1/2" rectangles

Dark Print Fabric:

#1—Cut 2—2-1/2" strips

#6—Cut 8—1-1/2" strips

#7—Cut 6—2" strips

Note: *Number these
strips as you cut.*

Make 25 Pieced Setting Blocks

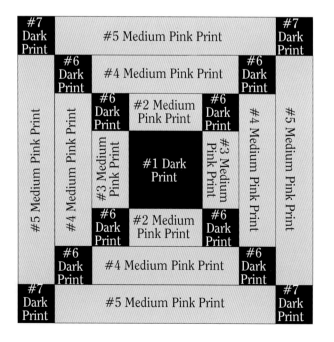

PIECING:

1 Sew a #2 medium pink print strip to each side of a #1 dark print strip. Press the seams toward the medium pink print. Make a total of two strip sets.

2 Cut each strip set into 16—2-1/2" x 4-1/2" units. You need 25 units.

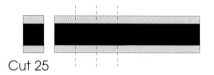

Cut 25

3 Sew a #6 dark print strip to each side of a #3 medium pink print strip. Press the seams toward the medium pink print. Make a total of two strip sets. Cut each strip into 26—1-1/2" x 4 -1/2" units. You need 50 units.

4 Sew one of these segments to each side of the center square units. This pieced square should measure 4-1/2".

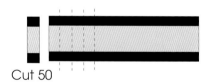

Cut 50

#6	#2	#6
#3	#1	#3
#6	#2	#6

5 Sew a #4 medium pink print rectangle to the opposite sides of the

pieced units. Press the seams toward the medium pink print.

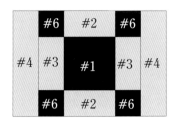

6 Sew a #6 dark print strip to each side of a #4 medium pink print strip. Press the seams toward the medium pink print. Make a total of two strip sets.

7 Cut each strip into 26—1-1/2" x 6-1/2" units. You need 50 units. Sew one of these segments to each side of the center-pieced units. This pieced unit should now measure 6-1/2".

Cut 50

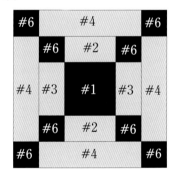

8 Sew a #5 medium pink print rectangle to the opposite sides of the center pieced units. Press the seams toward the medium pink print.

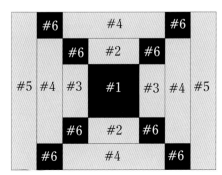

9 Sew a #7 dark print strip to each side of a #5 medium pink print strip. Press the seams toward the medium pink print fabric. Make a total of two strip sets.

10 Cut each strip into 20—2" x 9-1/2" units. You need 50 units. Sew one of these segments to each remaining side of the center-pieced units. The pieced setting blocks should now measure 9-1/2".

Cut 50

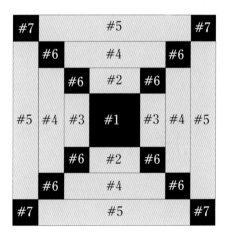

Note: *These pieced setting blocks have a built in "fudge factor". The #5 medium pink print rectangles and the #7 dark print squares are cut 1/2" wider than needed.*

As long as your seam allowances are consistent, the #5 medium print strips and the #7 dark print squares will all be trimmed to the same size.

The Quilt

QUILT CENTER:

1 Place the 8-1/2" *Square It Up & Fussy Cut* ruler on each setting block. The diagonal lines on the ruler should intersect the dark print squares. Trim all sides of the setting block.

2 Lay out the pieced setting blocks and the sashed Pieced Appliqué™ blocks so they have "eye appeal".

3 Sew these blocks together in seven rows of seven blocks. Press the seams toward the sashed Pieced Appliqué™ blocks.

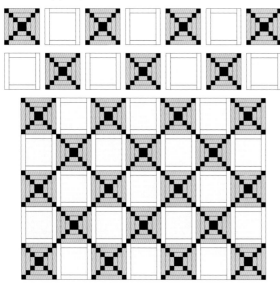

CUTTING
THE INNER AND OUTER BORDERS

Green Fabric:
Cut 6—2-1/2" strips
for the Inner Border

Floral Print Fabric:

Cut 4—7-1/2" x 76-1/2" strips
Cut strips the length of the
fabric, not the width for the
outer borders

Cut 4—2-1/2" x 76-1/2" strips
Cut strips the length of the
fabric, not the width for
the binding

INNER BORDER:

1 Trim the selvages from the 2-1/2" green inner border strips. Cut two of the strips in half.

2 Sew a half strip to each of the four remaining whole strips with a diagonal seam. Press these seams open.

3 Measure the top and bottom of the quilt center. Fit and sew one strip to the top of the quilt and one strip to the bottom of the quilt. Press the seams toward the inner border. Trim these strips even with the quilt center, if necessary.

4 Measure each side of the quilt center, including the top and bottom inner border strips. Fit and sew the two remaining pieced strips to each side of the quilt. Press the seams toward the inner border. Trim these strips even with the quilt center, if necessary.

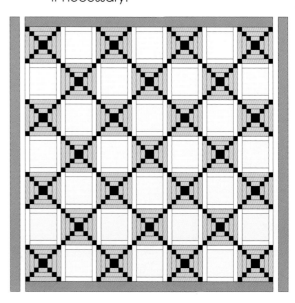

OUTER BORDER:

1 Sew a 7-1/2" x 76-1/2" floral print strip to the top and bottom of the quilt. The strips are longer than needed. Press the seams toward the outer border. Trim the strips even with the quilt center.

2 Sew a 7-1/2" x 76-1/2" floral print strip to each side of the quilt. The strips are longer than needed. Press the seams toward the outer border. Trim the strips even with the quilt center.

3 Quilt and bind as desired.

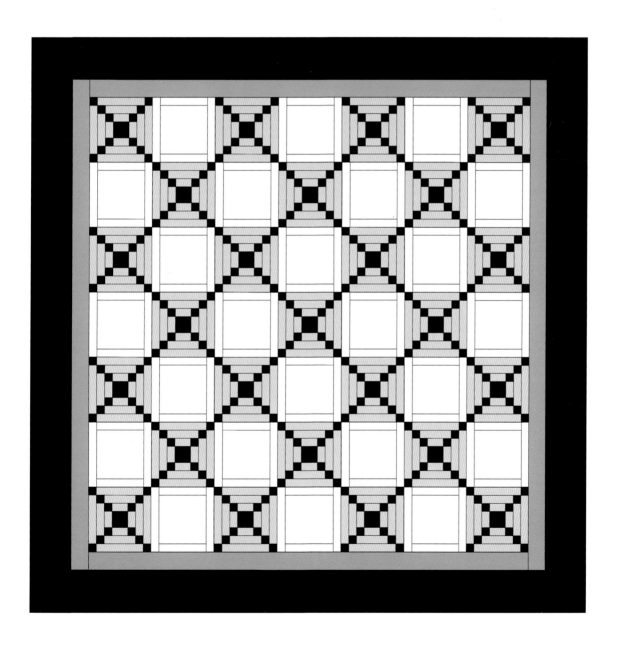

The Quilters

Front row, seated from left to right: Charlotte Smith, Mindy Kshywonis, Denise Edmunds, Helene Bednarczuk, and Cheryl Lorence.

Back row, standing from left to right: Deb Ambrus, Nada Garvin, Lynn Kraner, Jan Creekmore, Penny Haren, and Terrie Balthaser.

Not pictured: Jeanie Downey, Melanie Macdonald, Donna Garner, Rose Wetherill, and Stella Jordan.

Resources

Checker Distributors
400 W Dussel Dr Ste B
Maumee, OH 43537-1636
(800) 537-1060
www.checkerdist.com

Creative Grids®
www.creativegridsusa.com
c/o Checker Distributors
400 W. Dussel Drive, Suite B
Maumee, Ohio 43537-1636
1-800-537-1060

HQS, Inc.
P. O. Box 94237
Phoenix, AZ 85070-4237
(480)460-3697
www.trianglesonaroll.com

LakeHouse Dry Goods
www.lakehousedrygoods.com

Maywood Fabrics
E.E. Schenck Co.
6000 N. Cutter Circle
Portland, OR 97217
(800) 433-0722
OR
4561 Maywood Ave.
Vernon, CA 98858
(800) 237-6620
www.maywoodstudio.com

Penny Haren
www.pennyharen.com

Windham Fabrics
Baum Textile Mills, Inc.
812 Jersey Ave.
Jersey City, New Jersey 07310
(866) 842-7631
www.windhamfabrics.com